_____Devotions

_____for

_____Families

_____That

_____Can't

_____Sit

_____Still

DEVOTIONS
FOR FAMILIES

That Can't Sit Still

CAROLYN WILLIFORD

VICTOR BOOKS ®

A DIVISION OF SCRIPTURE PRESS PUBLICATIONS INC.
USA CANADA ENGLAND

Scripture quotations are from *New American Standard Bible,* © the Lockman Foundation 1960, 1962, 1963, 1968, 1971, 1972, 1973, 1975, 1977.

Library of Congress Cataloging-in-Publication Data

Williford, Carolyn.
   Devotions for families that can't sit still / by Carolyn Williford.
   p.   cm.
   Includes bibliographical references.
   ISBN: 0-89693-781-X
   1. Family—Prayer-books, devotions, etc.—English. I. Title.
II. Title: Devotions for families that cannot sit still.
   BV255.W49   1990
   249—dc20   89-48594
                                                      CIP

      3 4 5 6 7 8 9 10 Printing/Year 94 93 92 91

CONTENTS

For my family

Craig, Robb and Jay

*the cheerful subjects of my many "experiments"
and the recipients of my unconditional love*

C.Y.H.!

I have long shared Carolyn Williford's burden, as I too have desired to get God's Word into the lives, minds, and hearts of my four children. I have also shared Carolyn's disappointments, frustrations, and roadblocks along the way. From the standpoint of emotional, spiritual, and physical health, it is advantageous for children to have an early knowledge of God's truths for daily living, as they are given to us through His Word. That is why I am so excited about this book. It not only motivates parents in the area of family devotions for children, but it gives parents step-by-step instructions.

Devotions for school-age children *were* perplexing until now. Carolyn disposes of the myth that devotions have to be boring, repetitive, and dull. Preschool and school-age children are prime for learning God's Word. But when they are too old for cute stories and too young to understand deep theological truths, what do you do? This book provides some great ideas, but it can also be used as a catalyst to develop your own style of family devotions.

Carolyn shares from her own experiences so that each of these devotionals comes from the most thorough testing available—the Williford laboratory. What a labor of love—to provide fun, exciting devotions to teach your children why you desire for them to serve God. It does require commitment, planning, and preparation to equip your children with God's Word. But God's Word and your strong parental relationships will help them not want to stray far from His path as they venture out in life.

My advice to parents is to have fun with devotions and not be afraid to flop. Most important, get involved in your children's lives. Family devotions can be a bonding and building time of relationships between those in the family as well as with God.

God bless your venture to teach and train your children. It's an eternal investment well worth the time and effort you put forth.

Paul Meier, M.D.
Minirth-Meier Clinic
Richardson, Texas

As a Christian family, long ago my husband and I committed ourselves to spending regular devotional time with our children. From the time our sons were old enough to sit through (sort of) and participate in (after a fashion) a Bible story, question-and-answer time, favorite songs, and prayer on our knees together, we carried on a traditional nightly devotional time. When both advanced to school ages, however, this tradition became routine—and I mean *routine*, with all of its negative connotations: stale, repetitive, and unimaginative. We would grit our teeth with a "sit still while we enjoy this family time together" attitude. Obviously, a major change was needed if this tradition of family devotional time were to survive.

I remember very well the day our family devotions began to take on a totally new form. After spending my own time in God's Word and sincerely praying for our sons to grow into godly men, I felt strongly motivated to put much time and creative energy into a new devotional format. I suppose we could have continued our traditional approach, plodding through the teen years with a "normal" family devotional time. But urgent reasons for change kept nagging at the back of my mind—valid reasons to try a new approach. These considerations soon grew into convictions about the advantages of creative devotional times.

Making Eternal Investments

The Lord seemed to be saying to me, "You ask for godly sons, but what have *you* done today toward fulfilling this request?" I realized that my part in this responsibility was being pushed aside by the demands of the day, the hustle-bustle world that so often distracted me from what really counts. Eternal investments are generally not touchable, not measurable by human standards. Yet when I compare them with *earthly* investments, I find the true value of the eternal encourages and motivates me to plug on. So each week I determine to invest in my sons, for they have value beyond measure.

Creating Special Memories

In a taped message Dr. James Dobson relates that a pastor friend attended a conference of 25 to 30 pastors. Seated in a circle, they were asked to share memories of significant events in their lives. Dr. Dobson's friend noted that not *one* of the pastors shared his memories of family devotions. When he commented on this, the pastors agreed that they knew family devotions were important and necessary, but they considered them boring, monotonous, and something they wanted to get out of.[1] (When I played this tape, my younger son, who had been listening, *indignantly* responded, "Family devotions are *not* boring!")

I am determined that our family devotions will not suffer that same fate. Yes, traditional times of reading God's Word and praying together are important. But when this becomes a boring task performed out of duty—one our children wish to get out of—we *dare not* continue forcing them night after night. Think with me for a moment about the implications of this response to family devotions:

- Being with my family is no fun.
- Studying God's Word is boring.
- Christianity is not alive, real, or what life truly is all about.

I shudder to think that our children would ever consider our family devotions with these negative and damaging connotations.

Instead, my desire is for special memories, not a vague blur of boredom; positive experiences that we all look forward to, not another hurry-and-get-this-over-with type of evening; and finally, enriching times that connote the fun and sweetness of a hot fudge sundae, not a dutiful ritual reminiscent of spinach! (Apologies to the nutritionists and spinach growers.)

As Christian families, shouldn't our sweetest memories be the times we learned about and worshiped our God together? If not, don't we as parents have the responsibility to change this *now?*

Affirming Family Unity and Uniqueness

Family unity does not just automatically happen when a dad, mom, and children live in a house; it must be built, nurtured, and given quality time to become a reality in a home. We may not realize the need for family unity when children are small, but the teen years are just around the corner, and then the necessity for family support is *crucial.*

Dr. Merton Strommen conducted research by polling thousands of teens; his books, *Five Cries of Youth* and *Five Cries of Parents,* reveal startling facts about teens and their need for family support. He notes that:

> Adolescents in homes characterized by love and affectionate caring are better able to resist negative behaviors and more free to develop in positive ways. For instance, there is significantly less social alienation among adolescents whose parents emphasize nurturance, as well as less involvement in drug or alcohol use and sexual activity.[2]

Later he adds that "a close family characterized by parental affection, trust, doing things together, and strong support systems provides an inner resistance to the toxins of life."[3] From his questioning of teens, Dr. Strommen concludes that "the cry of these young people is 'I need to be part of a family where we love and accept and care about each other.'"[4]

As parents, we need to actively answer this cry for help. We cannot wait until the teen years to frantically race to meet these needs; *today* is when we must develop those crucial building blocks that will provide a firm foundation of support for the unsteady adolescent ages.

The glue of family unity is the knowledge that each member is unique in special God-given qualities, irreplaceable, and *needed* by the family for his or her contributions. Craig and I point out and emphasize these unique qualities often, giving our sons a self-worth based not on what they *do,* but on who they *are.* In a world that constantly focuses on the exterior—beauty, athletic abilities, intelligence and grades, wealth, popularity—Christian parents must counteract with praise for the eternal, inward qualities that God values.

One of our sons shows a tenderness toward others' feelings; we tell him God will use this for sensitivity in meeting needs. Our other son demonstrates strong personal discipline; we've pointed out that God will use his dedication to further His kingdom. By stressing that *no one* else could fill our family's needs with qualities just like these, we affirm our sons individually and promote family unity.

Family unity also contributes toward developing a family personality. We could be described as easygoing and fun-loving, yet also dedicated to knowing God and doing His will. We definitely do have a family character (pun intended) and that also gives us a sense of belonging, being comfortable with each other, and a unique bonding. However, we're still building—cementing block upon block, week by week. This type of structure—a supportive home—takes steady, committed workers. The payment is a closeness that's indescribable.

Making the Humdrum Special

Making a home sunny no matter how gloomy the day may be (due either to weather or circumstances) doesn't come easily. Parents have the special privilege and responsibility to demonstrate to their children that true joy does not depend on circumstances. Joy comes from our relationships with the Lord, and this is a constant. Therefore, I've made it my challenge to tackle life in a positive way through the good and bad, exciting and dull, holidays and everydays.

As Charles Swindoll has said, "We need to deliberately stop being absorbed by the details of life."[5] I strive to avoid being absorbed in everyday details by adding all the extra times that my family so enjoys—finding excuses for celebrations in nearly any situation. For instance, we celebrate all types of anniversaries, including one year in a new home. By making a special dessert (complete with candles and singing "Happy anniversary to us"), lighting a large family candle to share personal blessings from God over the past year, and then reminiscing about funny incidents, we've made what would have been an ordinary day *special.* Also, we have Father's Day and

Mother's Day, so why not a Children's Day? We like to commemorate this special occasion on the last day of school. Even our dog's birthday is cause for celebration—with cupcakes and ice cream, of course.

Continuing Commitment

Finally, the matter of *commitment* is most important. I realized that just as I was committed to my own personal devotions and the boys' individual devotions, I also needed to commit myself to family devotions that were meaningful—realizing that this would demand a greater time and energy input from me. I *am* committed to these family times together, for I see the beneficial outworkings in all of our lives; I am committed to *continuing* because I pray for a future harvest.

It is difficult to put time and energy into what can't be tangibly seen, measured, or even guaranteed for future gain. Still I am compelled to invest in family devotions for two very lovable (and loving), invaluable reasons: Robb and Jay. Knowing their Christian maturity is at stake, I need no further motivation.

Notes

1. James C. Dobson, The Spiritual Training of Children *(Focus on the Family, CS 063, 1987).*

2. Merton P. Strommen and A. Irene Strommen, Five Cries of Parents *(San Francisco: Harper and Row Publishers, 1985), pp. 94–95.*

3. Strommen and Strommen, p. 103.

4. Merton P. Strommen, Five Cries of Youth *(San Francisco: Harper and Row Publishers, 1979), p. 34.*

5. Charles R. Swindoll, "Leisure," Strengthening Your Grip *(Dallas: Word, Inc., 1983).*

One
GETTING THE MOST
FROM DEVOTIONAL TIMES

The 45 ideas in this book were all tested in the Williford laboratory. They'll get your devotional times off to a good start, and I think you'll be amazed at how much fun they are to plan and execute!

Eventually, though, you'll run out of planned ideas, or you'll feel a need for a devotional that fits your family specifically. For this reason you need to understand the philosophy behind these creative family devotions.

Our basic building block is *integration*. To integrate Christianity means essentially to allow it to touch, enter, and affect every aspect of life. I look through the "glasses" or grid of Christianity as I view my world, and thus my actions are (or should be) Christlike. Rather than a model of "We've read our devotional guide; now, let's go out into our world," I desire that our devotions model a living, practicing Christianity—an actual picture of the Christian lifestyle. We hope our sons recognize that we don't just *do* devotions; instead, we *live* Christianity every minute of the day. Thus these devotions are generally quite active—demonstrating the doing—and imitating the outworking of our Christian integration.

Also, I saw the struggles our sons were going through—rejection, loneliness, sportsmanship (or lack of it), making friends, being patient—and I would plan devotions designed to teach, encourage, convict, or bless, whichever was warranted for the situation. This way our devotions are often timely, meeting current needs as they arise. When I noticed a "me first" attitude growing, I planned the Servant Jar Week; later a season of basketball league would prompt Good Sports Night. Again my prayer was that we all realize our Christianity is what we *live*, and specifically what we live *today*.

(Disclaimer: In no way do we intend to claim that a devotional on good sportsmanship will totally cure a child's temper after losing a game, nor will the Servant Jar miraculously transform every member of the family into a considerate helper every minute of the day. These devotions *are* intended as teaching tools, guides, and helps to facilitate growth in our Christian development.)

Lastly, I often attempt to incorporate the boys' current fascinations, fads, or acquirements into our devotions. When they received a laser tag game, we used it to shoot Goliath (see "Killing Giants"). If your children enjoy different types of building blocks, they can construct a number of things: a model of the temple, Noah's ark, a Tower of Babel (the possibilities seem endless). When the Olympics commanded our attention, we followed suit, competing in the Williford Olympics—which included everything from sit-ups to video game rivalries. I guess our philosophy is that it seems senseless to fight *against* what currently absorbs our sons' attention; instead, we attempt to *use* these things they enjoy to capture their interest in devotions.

We've learned much these last several years—sometimes what *not* to do as well as what *to do.* I share the remaining suggestions with you in hope that you may benefit from our goofs and successes.

Plan Ahead

When we first started in full-time ministry, Craig would leave his night off blank on his weekly planning calendar. Then if someone called and needed an appointment, he would quickly scan his schedule, note the empty night, and write in another meeting. Oops! Another family night would disappear! He soon learned (translation: nagging reminders hit brain matter) that a family night was equally important as other appointments. Thus, he purposefully writes on his calendar "family night" and treats it just like any other scheduled meeting.

After planning one night a week as our family time together, I then must set aside time to plan what we're going to do. One lesson we definitely have learned: quality family nights do not just happen. If we have not purposefully planned an evening, it seems to just drift away . . . into extra coffee for Craig and me, playing for the boys, and that one-eyed monster every family wrestles with: television. Assuming we will have a worthwhile family devotion just because we're together is a real temptation, but unfortunately, that is a false thesis.

Another element to planning is being prepared, and thus I try to have all our needed materials collected and available beforehand. After we had several devotionals with this new format, I realized that we used certain supplies often; therefore, I have attempted to keep these in stock around the house. With these materials already handy, my preparation time is much more efficient. In the section entitled "Basic Instructions," you'll find a list of items to begin collecting now.

Set Realistic Goals

As already stated, we plan a devotional once a week. When our children were small, we read and sang together nearly every night. Now, however, they are much more active in events outside the home: weekly Awana, musical groups (choirs, handbells, cantata rehearsals), Bible workshops or studies, and various other activities. These are, in our estimation, extremely valuable experiences. To plan devotions on these nights would be to fight against them; instead, since they all contribute to our sons' spiritual growth, we encourage their involvement. Therefore, we set a realistic goal for our family to meet together around God's Word once a week.

Other families (especially those with younger children), however, may be able to have family devotions much more often. The key is to decide on a *realistic* number of nights a week. Again, planning on too much sets us up for failure, guilt, and eventual loss of any devotional family time at all. Each family—and only that family—can decide on the right number of evenings (or mornings or afternoons) per week that is realistic and workable for that family.

Be Flexible

When I discussed earlier how to plan ahead by putting "family night" on the calendar, I made that sound so easy, didn't I? Right. Unfortunately, interruptions and emergencies do happen, and these can be frustrating and discouraging. But we are slowly learning that *flexibility* is a key element. No, the wonderful night that was planned does not always come to pass; other times what I thought would be a terrific idea is a major flop. If I'm rigid in what I expect—"once a week no matter what and the devotional must be wonderful"—I'm setting us up for failure.

If I can be flexible, expecting plans to fall through sometimes and other great ideas to go sour, I can survive and continue. We have learned, for example, that a serious devotional when the boys are in a giggling mood is just not going to be in *any* way a positive experience! As a matter of fact, we've found that we're right back to the "We're *going* to enjoy this . . ." through gritted teeth scenario! Instead, we'll be flexible and play an active game when they obviously need an outlet to expend extra energy. And yes, there are still times when a devotional bombs. But I think surfacing hidden expectations ("every devotional will be wonderful") and allowing for flexibility (three "Sit still's!" during supper mean a change in plans) can protect us from devotional burnout.

Allow for "Just Plain Fun"

Our devotions do include serious worship times—dedications, consecrations, and holiday traditions when we share while holding candles which provide low lighting to help set a mood of reverence and worship. Our sons also know that prayertime must be respectful as we approach our holy God. These solemn moments of reverent worship have given our family an undercurrent of fortified kinship, a spiritual bonding that's indescribable. I cherish my memories of these devotions and anxiously look forward to many more.

Other family nights combine Scripture applications with a good dose of fun. Where did we pick up the idea that devotions must always be *serious?* Who said we have to sit still? Why can't we be creative? And heaven forbid that we might even laugh! We believe that an element of fun is important, and the benefit of this has been that our kids truly enjoy and look forward to our family night. However, please note that this *does not* mean our devotions have no substance. Content and substance can be communicated in a fun way, and most of our devotions fall into this category.

The third type of family night we sometimes share is, essentially, just plain fun. We've had scavenger hunts, clue quests, silly shoe games, two-on-two sport games, indoor table games, etc. In other words, we *play* together. No agenda. We just want to enjoy being together and enjoy the beautiful gift of life that God has given us. Again, however, please realize that these times are constantly infused with teachable moments. What better time can there be for modeling and teaching sportsmanship—being a gracious winner, building the self-image of the awkward child, encouraging *team* rather than *star* tactics—than when actually playing with a child? Parents have the opportunity to integrate countless lessons during quality interaction.

In addition to teachable moments, family fun helps us all *laugh* together. Health specialists tell us that laughter acts as a positive release for stress, helping the whole body to recover. We've found that laughter has amazing healing powers for our family too. It provides joyful memories, promotes bonding through genuine friendships, and unites us in love. Contrary to the old saying, everything that's good for us doesn't *have* to hurt!

Build Interest and Cooperation
When teaching classes on this type of family devotions, we have been asked, "How do you get your kids to *do* all of these things?" Frankly, that has not been a serious problem. As I mentioned, we do have our flops; every Williford is not always a happy camper. Yet there is generally a spirit of cooperation because of several factors, some inherent and others that came about through conscious effort.

First, Craig and I attempt to model genuine, excited interest. Being genuine is extremely important; kids easily spot a phony. Therefore, we strongly recommend attempting only that which you as parents are genuinely interested in. If we approach devotions with disinterest or a bored attitude, our children will respond likewise. Of course, having the energy to approach devotions with excitement is a major factor. Therefore, planning our family nights on a day that we know will be physically or emotionally exhausting is obviously not a wise idea. Even the best planning can be negated, though, by unexpected work loads, sickness, or just plain worn-out moms and dads. That's when it's time to be flexible; don't attempt an ambitious family night without that needed energy and excitement.

Craig and I inherently enjoy games; we like the activity, competition, and enthusiasm of playing with our boys. However, I grew up loving to play with dolls, doll clothes, and doll paraphernalia. I now have two boys. It should come as no surprise that I am now surrounded by every sort of ball imaginable, cars, trucks, airplanes, and war toys. Obviously, I had to make some major adjustments. I do not inherently enjoy playing catcher for my guys' baseball practice (nor would any T-ball league in town draft me for my abilities), but I *do* play because I want to be with my family, actively participating. We parents must motivate ourselves to do that which we inherently enjoy *and* that which we do not. Our principal motivation is the extremely valuable benefits our children will receive.

Also, we've noticed that our kids will follow our lead. Sometimes that translates into off-the-wall activities, like yelling "This family is crazy!" (outside, by the way) as one of the requirements for our scavenger hunt; other times it translates into imitating us, like leaving thoughtful surprises (cards, candy bars, notes of encouragement) for a Secret Pal when we drew each others' names. After seeing creative ideas demonstrated, the boys have then amazed Craig and me with their innovation and desire to contribute in imaginative ways. Now on Kid's Night, when they are in charge of devotions, the boys' originality puts ours to shame.

Past experiences compel me to add a word here on competition. Somewhere between the ages of 7 to 11, children enter a highly competitive phase. Losing a game is equated with rejection, loneliness, and a loss of security in self-image. Therefore, we have found that we must use any competition in games very carefully, avoiding any stress or the appearance of threat to one's worth or position within the family. When a devotional is a disaster because of a disconsolate loser, we've found that it's a great idea to schedule a "self-image builder" devotional right away.

Don't Let Guilt Get in the Way

I wonder how many families have begun devotions, missed some due to inevitable scheduling problems, and then not resumed them because of guilt. Why is it so hard to start again what we were once so excited about? Guilt should be a productive experience, bringing about constructive changes. But too often guilt results in a negative hindering, paradoxically keeping us from doing what we intended to do. When we miss a family devotion time, we decide *not* to allow guilt to hinder or diminish our commitment. We just plan on trying again next week. And if next week gets lost in the shuffle too (as often happens during special weeks—vacations, for example), I just begin again, and again, and again.

Discover Good Literature

As an English teacher, I have a profound appreciation for well-written books. I could list the components that the gifted author demonstrates, but that's not necessary when we finish an exceptional book. We all recognize a good story. Authors like C.S. Lewis, Madelaine L'Engle, and David and Karen Mains have kept our family members engrossed in their books. We've traveled into outer space, allegorical fantasies, and Narnia in our imaginations, and we have found there much to think about and thoroughly enjoy. I highly recommend reading good literature for devotions, and be sure to stop in the middle of the most exciting part. (Teachers do this. It drives children crazy, but they *beg* for more!)

Build on Prayer

The foundation, guide, and bonding point of our family devotions is prayer. I like to think of it as a saturation process. I ask for wisdom beforehand to know what God would have us do; we ask that He would use the devotional to meet our family's needs; and finally, holding hands in a circle, we pray for each other and those for whom we feel concern.

I believe that our children can pray more sincerely—and thus more effectively—for people if they know or can relate to them. Therefore, Craig and I will choose prayer requests that they can understand or ones which we can explain to them before we begin praying. To pray for "Jane Doe" doesn't mean much to a child *or* an adult; to pray for Mrs. Brown's broken leg because "I've broken a bone before and know how much it hurts and how inconvenient it is" makes quite a difference in the sincerity of all our prayers.

An important part of our family prayertime is sharing personal needs and requests. After deciding who will pray for whom, I love hearing the boys pray for Dad, me, or each other. That's music to a mom's ears when brothers were arguing just an hour ago. There is a special bonding that takes place when a group prays together, and I pray this bonding will continue through the ups and downs of the teen years and on into the boys' future homes as they establish their own family traditions.

How to Adapt Devotions for Age Differences

In general, these devotions are applicable for the elementary years, ages 5 through 12. Our sons were 6 and 9 when we first began experimenting with this new devotional format; they are now 9 (and three quarters, according to him) and 12, and our family times have changed and adapted well with their growth. It will be interesting to see how our devotions change as both become teens.

An appropriate time to begin this type of format would be when a child is about five or six. In our experience, this was the age at which our children became bored with the repetitive reading and singing. School introduces experiences which help children grow in a number of areas: cooperation in group activities, fine motor coordination for handling crayons and pencils, gross motor coordination for various active games, and working with language, reading, and writing. These various skills are important to this type of family devotion. When adapting these devotions for children from ages 5 to 12, parents must ask themselves some important questions about their children's attention spans and abilities.

First, ask yourself, *How long is my child's attention span?* In other words, how long can he or she sit, listen, and learn? If you have two, three, or more children, how will you adjust times? Obviously, young children just cannot pay attention or absorb as much as the older child. Important clue: look for the signs. When children begin wiggling more than they are listening, poking little brother, or asking what's for dinner tomorrow, time is up. Remember that *mood* is also to be taken into account. When our children reach the "perpetual giggle" stage, they are past the point of educational benefit. (We have also learned that's when we find out how much patience Mom and Dad possess.)

Next ask, *What abilities by ages do my children demonstrate?* Knowing and understanding age-related abilities can be helpful in planning devotions for our families, so I offer the following information for a guide.

Ages 5–7—Children at this stage of development have a limited understanding of time; thus, the promise of a trip to the beach next year means little to a five-year-old. He can't grasp the concept of "next year." They also cannot understand concepts or application of illustrations. To talk to a child in this age category about "combating giants in our lives" (illustrating an application from David and Goliath) would just be confusing. But memorizing Scripture (even that which they cannot fully comprehend), acting out Bible stories in charades or skits, or making musical instruments for praise *are* activities within their abilities. Children of this age need to focus on one thing at a time (thus repetition—in various styles and using different tools—is helpful); they're self-centered (did we parents need to be told *that?*); and they're very curious—a great quality for teachability.

Ages 7–11—Somewhere in this age range children begin to conceptualize, and this is when the possibilities for application really begin. And what possibilities! We can use our creative energy to visualize as we take children from the specific to the general. A cocoon can provide a wonderful illustration of how to help children apply concepts. By demonstrating a *normal* cocoon and a *helped* cocoon (helping the moth causes it to die), we illustrate—visually and graphically—how and why God chooses not to do the maturing process *for* His children. Strength comes through struggle. Also, remember that children within these ages need organized, concrete, and literal illustrations to teach generalizations. That's why advanced preparation is so important and visual aids of all varieties are helpful. Repeat these applications in many ways to insure that they do grasp the concept being taught.

Most of these devotions can be adapted for younger or older children, depending on a family's needs. Even dialoguing (talking about our feelings on a particular subject) can be done by children who cannot yet write. Our children drew pictures that represented their feelings (as did Mom and Dad); now that we're long past the need for drawing, our kids still insist on an illustration. It seems that they view the drawing as a major part of the fun. (If you have an older toddler, put him or her in a high chair with a crayon to create a "lovely" picture too.)

Please feel free to adapt, stretch, or use these devotions as a springboard to create your own times together. Just as we are a unique and God-designed family, so is your family. Our prayer is that these devotions will bring out the specialness with which you have been blessed.

Basic Instructions

Though many of the devotions in this book do not fit any general pattern, most do follow a common progression. This order developed in part because of our concern for quality educational experiences and also because of children's inherent enjoyment of repetitive patterns. Our kids feel comfortable with and like this order; part of their enthusiasm seems to be their anticipation of the expected fun! The basic pattern we follow is this:

1. *Short prayer first*—Beginning with a long prayer or asking for prayer requests at this time just doesn't work for us. The kids are generally too keyed-up for concentration or concern for others to have a quality time in prayer. Thus, we share only a short prayer at the beginning, asking God to direct our time together.

2. *Bible reading*—This comes next because their ability to sit still and listen for details is the highest at this time. (Please note that the opening prayer has set an atmosphere of "It's time to settle down now.") Any major points that we want to impress on them are made here, for later they'll be much too wiggly to absorb the heavier information.

3. *Activities*—Saving the most exciting activities for last is always a must. We have found that once the boys are in high gear, there is virtually no way to then return to a calm, instructional type of teaching (except for getting out the "board of education," which we try to avoid at all costs during devotions). It is really unfair to expect this of children; they just can't switch gears as quickly as adults.

4. *Closing prayer*—Though our boys may be excited from the preceding activities, they have learned to adapt to our pattern of closing prayer. Focusing on spiritual principles during the devotion seems to have made an impression concerning the importance of prayer. Yes, sometimes we do find that we must

cut this time shorter than we'd like because they are not concentrating. Most of the time, however, their prayers reflect an understanding and personal application of what we have just learned together. We also use this time to share prayer requests and pray for each other, which is a real bonding experience for us as a family.

Materials Needed

Earlier I spoke of the many materials I keep handy for future use in our devotions. Since I use these items constantly, keeping them in supply eliminates running to the store each week. Therefore, I suggest you begin collecting them now, and replenish supplies as you use them:

- notebook paper
- felt-tip pens (all colors, broad and fine points)
- crayons
- yarn, string
- construction paper (all colors)
- 3" x 5" file cards
- Scotch Tape and masking tape
- modeling clay
- poster board
- cardboard
- candles
- shoe boxes
- crepe paper
- Christian music—adult/children—tapes, records, etc.
- assorted "junk"—paper towel tubes, plastic baskets, Popsicle sticks, empty jars, anything that looks like it has creative possibilities.

Construction Tips

Some may be frightened at the prospect of making or constructing the various items for these devotions. But rest assured, you need not be an artist to have successful results. Most of all, your children will appreciate your efforts, time, and especially the fun benefits they will receive. So be creative, colorful, and most important for your sake, enjoy yourself!

For nearly every devotion, I make what I have termed a "table marker." On two 3″ x 5″ cards, I write out with felt-tip pens, (using different colors for variety) the verses that pertain to our study. Sometimes I use the same verse on both cards; other times I put different verses on each card. Using a third card as the base, I bend and tape the cards to form what looks like a triangle. (See illustration below.) This then displays the verses for a centerpiece on the dinner table that night. We have found this to be a successful way to introduce our devotional's topic and begin asking pertinent questions. The kids have turned this tradition into their own form of guessing game: they quiz us to find out what we're doing that night. Believe me, that doesn't bother us one bit, for their questions achieve one of our goals—getting them *interested!*

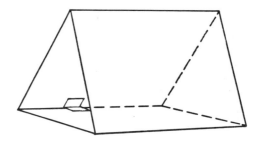

The Key to Your Motivation

I wish that there were some magical phrase, a stirring combination of words that would compel you as parents to commit to attempting family devotions. Unfortunately, I do not believe such literary expertise exists. But I hope that you have captured some of our dedication, excitement, and determination to invest in what we consider invaluable: our sons' Christian growth.

We also have a fervent yearning to minister to families. We experience heartfelt pain for the child who desperately desires attention from his too-busy parents; for the family racing all different directions to keep up with activities with no time for each other; for the college students we have ministered to who commented, with genuine yearning in their voices, "*We* never did anything like that as a family." We desire to somehow encourage family members' finding support in each other in this disheartening, devastating world and to provide hope for those families who have forgotten how to enjoy each other.

We offer this book with counsel and practical suggestions for those of you who already are on this bumpy and pothole-filled road named Commitment to Family Time. The destructive elements of stress, time pressure, and mixed-up priorities constantly threaten to detour us. Once on this road, it's just as difficult to remain there. Some may consider family devotions unnecessary, believing that because they're Christian they will glide safely through life. Our complacency is dangerous, especially when our children's lives are at stake.

When my sons were little and one came running with a scraped knee, I found that a kiss, hug, and Band-Aid quickly soothed all injuries. I remember musing to myself during those years, "Oh, if only all the hurts of their older years could be cured so easily." Now I know that hurts can't be easily erased, nor should I even attempt to alleviate some, for they are God's molding toward maturity. Yet I can attempt to provide a home that is a safe harbor, a joyful community of love and worship of our Lord, a nurturing preparation for the big, harsh world that's right outside our door.

Please join us in worshiping as a family. Our children still get injuries (but more on the *inside* now), the hurts that tear at their self-worth and can crush hopes and dreams. Now their tender *hearts* cry for a kiss, hug, and Band-Aid—an atmosphere conducive to healing. Lord, may our family worship provide just that.

> Why do you call me, "Lord, Lord," and do not do what I say? I will show you what he is like who comes to Me and hears My words and puts them into practice. He is like a man building a house, who dug down deep and laid the foundation on rock. When a flood came, the torrent struck that house but could not shake it, because it was well built. But the one who hears My words and does not put them into practice is like a man who built a house on the ground without a foundation. The moment the torrent struck that house, it collapsed and its destruction was complete. (Luke 6:46-49)

Two
BIBLE STORIES

KILLING GIANTS

MATERIALS NEEDED:
- [ ] Bible
- [ ] poster board
- [ ] laser tag guns, target (You may substitute another type of gun and target such as dart board and rubber-tipped darts, rubber bands, or even tiddledywinks!)
- [ ] felt-tip pens
- [ ] 3″ x 5″ cards
- [ ] construction paper (white)
- [ ] tape
- [ ] pencils
- [ ] scissors

TEXT: 1 Samuel 17

PREPARATION:

[ ] Draw a large Goliath on poster board. Draw an outline of a small Goliath on construction paper. Trace one for each member of the family and cut out one for each person. Or make photocopies of the Goliaths on page 33, and cut them out. Paste the large Goliath on a piece of poster board.

[ ] Construct table marker, if desired. You might want to write out just the first part of 1 Samuel 17:1: "Now the Philistines gathered their forces for war." Then, do some research concerning battles, weapons, and armor for this period of history. (Consult the

list of resources at the back of this book.)

☐ Study 1 Samuel 17.

☐ Set up the large poster-board Goliath so that he leans against a chair. Place the target (laser target or dart board) behind or above Goliath so that you will be shooting at him. (If you are using rubber bands, you can just shoot at Goliath himself.) Make sure guns are ready and working; test by shooting target.

FAMILY TIME:

1. Open with prayer.

2. Read aloud 1 Samuel 17. Draw attention to David's courage in the face of a huge foe and seemingly impossible battle. Discuss what foe (or any problem in our way) is too big for God—or is there any? Does this also apply to us today? Ask: **What happens when we concentrate on the size of the problem?** (It seems mighty big!) **What happens when we concentrate instead on the size of our God?** (The problem gets smaller and more manageable.)

3. Allow each family member to shoot Goliath with laser gun, darts, or rubber bands.

4. Discuss how, just like David, we also have battles against foes or problems. Parents, share struggles that you have, like loving the unlovable coworker, not being grumpy when the schedule is hectic, etc. Be honest, sincere, and truthful; your sharing will draw out concerns from your children. (If necessary, use questions to guide them: "How's it going on the playground? What about that classmate who was teasing you? Are you getting along better with your teacher?")

5. Hand out small Goliaths and pencils.

6. Have each person write his or her present main struggle on the Goliath.

7. Everyone should then exchange Goliaths and pray for the person and the problem represented by that Goliath.

8. Remind everyone that family members will continue praying for each other about these concerns.

SUGGESTIONS:

First, this devotional calls for application abilities; therefore, only older children (ages seven and up) could understand this concept.

(You must decide if your seven- or eight-year-old has the ability needed.) If your children are younger, be patient; you have plenty of time to use this in later years.

We did this because the laser tag game was a recent gift with which the whole family was currently fascinated. I began considering ways to put this interest to work for a family time, and thus while recalling famous battles, I naturally thought of David and Goliath. Goliath then became the target of our shooting, and the application would be how we battle giants in our spiritual warfare just as David did. Be sure to point out that, with God's help, we have the power to *defeat* these foes.

Our sharing and prayertime was meaningful too. The boys seemed willing to reveal their current struggles. They had no trouble comprehending what a "giant" represented and quickly identified their own giants. I also noticed a concern for each other during the prayertime. Because we had shared openly, our prayers could be more specific and significant.

Just remember, parents, you must set an example by being open first. If you do not reveal heartfelt struggles, but instead offer mere pat phrases, your children will most likely respond the same way. And note that this also presupposes that you are *in* the battle and aware of your weaknesses—something you may need to prayerfully consider first.

"LIVE" INTERVIEW

MATERIALS NEEDED:
- [ ] Bible
- [ ] "microphone"—an adapted jump rope handle, wooden spoon, or possibly a mike from a cassette recorder
- [ ] costumes, if desired (bathrobes, scarves, and rope ties to imitate biblical times) for three men; dress clothes for the interviewer

TEXT: Daniel 3 (You may want to read Daniel 1 and 2 for background on Daniel and King Nebuchadnezzar.) Make sure that you emphasize to your children that it was *God's power* that protected the men in the furnace; their faith sustained them, but *God* gave them the faith.

PREPARATION:
- [ ] Determine which of your family members can best perform the roles of the interviewer (the parent putting together this devotion should probably take this role) and Shadrach, Meshach, and Abed-nego. (Others in the family? Or little ones? An audience to perform for would be great!)
- [ ] Have costumes and microphone ready.
- [ ] Construct table marker, if desired. Write out just part of Daniel 3:28: "They trusted in Him and defied the king's command and were willing to give up their lives rather than serve or worship any god except their own God."

FAMILY TIME:

1. During dinner, read the table marker and introduce the night's topic by asking: **Can you guess which biblical characters this is referring to? What kind of faith in God would this require? Could *you* do this?** (If your children bring up other biblical characters, don't discourage them. Instead, use the opportunity to discuss those people of God also. Then lead the discussion back to Daniel and his friends.)

2. Open with prayer.

3. Read Daniel 3 (or chapters 1–3 if your children are older). As

you are reading, use voice inflection to emphasize details and bring the story alive. Your excitement will help later as everyone takes on his or her character.

4. Announce that the family is going to role play a live interview with Shadrach, Meshach, and Abed-nego which takes place just after their experience in the furnace. Assign the roles as you judge best fit your family. (If costumes are used, allow time here for everyone to get changed.) Mention a recent interview which your family has seen or heard on TV or radio; this will help to set the mood that is needed.

5. As in a play, arrange the characters and audience (if you have one) so that the interviewer can proceed. The interviewer should begin just as a live interview does:

> "Ladies and gentlemen, we're here live in Babylon to report to you the amazing details of what appears to be a miracle! We are fortunate to have the opportunity to interview—*live*—three men who actually survived—believe it or not— being thrown into a fiery furnace! Shadrach, can you tell us . . . ?"

6. You may want to consider using some of these questions:
- **In your opinion, just what has happened here?**
- **What were you feeling when the king made his decree? When you disobeyed? When you knew you would be thrown into the furnace? When you saw another Man in the fire? What do you feel now?**
- **Has this experience changed you somehow? How about your faith?**
- **Would you advise others to do the same thing?**
- **What has this taught you about God?**
- ***Could* you have faced this ordeal without God's help?**

Be sure to alternate to whom your questions are addressed. If one character is uncooperative (you may hear some "I dunno's"), just move on to another. Adapt questions for the age of the child you are addressing, saving more intuitive questions for the older child or the parent. Wrap up your interview with a short testimony, sharing how *you* have been changed by this miracle of God.

7. Close with prayer, thanking God for the evidence of His power in the lives of family members. Try to specify an instance of this in your recent past.

SUGGESTIONS:

The success of this devotion will largely depend on the interviewer and his or her ability to "get into" the role—or in other words, to *ham it up!* The interviewer must have plenty of excitement and energy to bring this off, so attempt this on a night when this is possible.

We enjoyed this unique format because the story seemed to come alive for our kids. Through this technique, they realized that this event *actually happened.* Though it is a tongue-in-cheek approach, the format did not lessen the impact of the account. Instead, by role playing these godly men, the boys seemed to gain new insight, understanding, and appreciation for the courage and faith demonstrated by Shadrach, Meshach, and Abed-nego.

PARABLES

MATERIALS NEEDED:
- ☐ Bible
- ☐ paper, pen
- ☐ pictures for illustration, if desired

TEXT: Matthew 13

PREPARATION:

☐ Read Matthew 13. Decide which parable is appropriate for your children's age-levels. Consult your Bible notes or resource list for explanations. Practice reading the parable aloud.

☐ Write your own parable (an illustrative story about humans or nature which teaches us about God). I would advise using animals rather than people since children relate so well to animals and will enjoy the "make-believe" and yet *applicable* quality animals provide. Be sure to make use of animals which your children are particularly interested in—such as dogs, cats, or even dinosaurs! Our parable went like this:

A Puppy Named Woot

Once there was a very cute and cuddly pup named Woot. His owner loved him dearly and taught him many tricks and also several rules because he loved his puppy and did not want him to be harmed. For example, the owner taught Woot never, never, never to cross the street because a car would certainly crush Woot flat. So Woot learned his rules and obeyed his owner, and he was a very happy puppy.

One day, however, all Woot's neighborhood friends came over to play—a cocker spaniel named Buffy, a Shih Tzu named KoKo, and a big mutt named Scruffy. Scruffy announced excitedly that there was a big box of spilled dog biscuits on the other side of the road—big, delicious, yummy dog biscuits just waiting for them to go gobble them up! Buffy and KoKo agreed that this was a splendid opportunity, and they all looked to Woot to see if he agreed. Woot had a definite problem. For crossing the road was a big "no-no."

Still, all his friends urged him to go, and all those yummy biscuits were just sitting there, waiting for them. What harm would come from crossing the road just *once*? Woot agonized about what to do and finally decided *not* to disobey his owner; he would not cross the road.

Woot's friends, however, were determined to go without him. Woot held his breath as the three stepped onto the road and proceeded across.

So you want to know how this story ends? Well, you might think that the dogs were killed by a car. But no, not *one* was harmed at all. As a matter of fact, they chowed down those yummy biscuits and came back across the road safely to taunt Woot for being so silly! Why, they had actually been rewarded for breaking the rule! It all seemed so very, very unfair to poor Woot, so he began to ponder about this experience. Here are some of the questions he asked himself:

1. Should I have crossed the road?

2. The other dogs disobeyed the rule, so why weren't they punished? Why did they receive rewards when they disobeyed?

3. I obeyed the rule; why didn't I get rewarded? Or was I rewarded, in another way?

4. It was very, very difficult for me to not cross the road when all my friends did. What if this happens again? (What could we tell Woot to encourage him to continue to obey the rule?)

5. What about the rule? Is it a good one? Why did my owner make this rule?

FAMILY TIME:

1. Open with prayer.

2. Describe what a parable is and read an example from Matthew 13. (Explain what the parable means.)

3. Explain that you have written a make-believe parable, and ask family members to listen carefully to the story.

4. Discuss possible applications. (Ours included discussing how we resist when we are pressured to do something wrong—especially when those doing the wrong are rewarded. We talked about

which types of rewards are more important, and how we can encourage each other when events like this happen).

5. Discuss prayer requests which relate to the parable.

6. Pray for each other.

SUGGESTIONS:

This type of devotion serves two functions: first, it teaches about parables—what they are and how Christ used them—and second, the subject matter of the parable can be applied to any problem areas that you want to teach your children without *lecturing them.* And this is the strength of a story—especially one that involves characters which deeply interest your children. Your points will come across much more effectively, and no "finger wagging" will be needed!

Keep in mind these two cautions: first, the parable that you choose from the Bible and the one that you write should be appropriate for your children's ages. Because our sons were older when we did this, we included deeper concepts. Second, for younger children the old adage of "keeping it simple" is important here; they'll retain *more* if you teach *less.*

BIBLE CHARADES

MATERIALS NEEDED:
- ☐ Bible
- ☐ costumes and props, if desired

TEXT: Use any Bible stories that your children know well and that are suitable for acting out. We have done these:
- Exodus 2:1-8 (Moses' birth and adoption by Pharaoh's daughter)
- Exodus 3:1-21 (Moses before the burning bush)
- Joshua 5:13–6:27 (Joshua and the fall of Jericho)
- 1 Samuel 3:1-21 (the Lord's calling of Samuel)
- 1 Samuel 20 (Jonathan's demonstration of love and commitment to David)
- 2 Kings 4:8-37 (the raising of the Shunammite woman's son)
- 2 Kings 5:1-14 (Naaman healed of leprosy)
- Daniel 3 (Shadrach, Meshach, and Abed-nego)
- Luke 2:1-20 (Jesus' birth)
- Matthew 8:23-27 (Jesus calms the sea)
- Matthew 14:13-21 (Jesus feeds 5,000 people)
- Matthew 14:22-32 (Peter walks on water)
- Luke 10:38-41 (Jesus with Mary and Martha)
- Luke 18:15-17 (Jesus loving little children)
- Luke 19:1-9 (the story of Zaccheus)
- John 11:1-44 (Jesus raises Lazarus from the dead)
- Mark 16:1-8 and John 20:1-18 (the empty tomb)

PREPARATION:
- ☐ Decide which passages are suitable for your children— taking into consideration their ages and abilities.
- ☐ Gather necessary props and costumes, if desired.

FAMILY TIME:
1. Open with prayer.
2. Explain that you're going to play a fun and active new game: acting out Bible stories! Divide into two teams; each team chooses several passages to portray.

3. Take turns presenting your plays, with one team guessing what story from the Bible the other is portraying. (NOTE: Be sure to finish each skit, even if the guessing team does correctly identify the passage.)

4. Sit in a circle for closing prayer, thanking God for His Word and family fun.

SUGGESTIONS:

Children of all ages will love this type of devotion, for they can participate fully (by suggesting stories, acting them out, and guessing too), and they are actually *encouraged* to wiggle those active little bodies. Not much sitting still for this devotional! Encourage their active participation by being open to the stories they are familiar with. The passages suggested here may be helpful as starting points, but be sure to allow *them* the freedom to choose stories they know.

We have repeated this family worship many times, for it comes in handy when the boys are especially animated, when we have guests who wish to participate, or whenever we feel a need to work out some of the day's stresses. We've even found this to be a great party activity.

If you do not have enough members in your family to divide into teams, you can still act out the stories. We used to do this with our children when they were very little. They would beg to do it nearly every night, and we would consent when we had sufficient energy!

Children benefit greatly from hearing the Bible story and then having it reinforced through role playing. And Mom and Dad, *you* will benefit greatly from time well spent with your children.

Three
GOD'S WORD

FAMILY MEMORIZATION

MATERIALS NEEDED:
- [ ] Bible
- [ ] 3" x 5" file cards
- [ ] felt-tip pens
- [ ] paper, pens

TEXT: Galatians 5:22-23 (for a shorter text) or Psalm 46—or another psalm you may think appropriate (for a longer text)

PREPARATION:

[ ] Decide which passage best suits your family for memorization. You may want to choose a text that was not listed here, especially if you desire one for a specific need your family has. For example, if your children have specific fears that you wish to help them conquer, you may want to choose Joshua 1:9. Consult the back of your Bible for helps or look through a concordance to find specific concepts.

[ ] Divide the passage into equal parts or, if you have a disparity in ability to memorize because of age differences, divide the passage according to those abilities.

[ ] Write each person's name and the section he or she is to memorize on a 3" x 5" card with colorful marking pens. (Suggestion: Give mom or dad the first part of the verse. This way one of you can be responsible for *starting* the recitation over and over as you bike or hike.)

☐ On paper, write out a "contract" for each person; ours looked like this:

I, _____(name)_____ , agree to work on memorizing to the best of my ability _____(Scripture passage)_____ on this day of _____(date)_____ .

_____
signature

☐ Plan a bike ride or hike together, if possible.

FAMILY TIME:

1. Open with prayer.

2. Discuss how, as a family, you are going to memorize a portion of Scripture. Emphasize that this will not be hard because each person has a section, and it won't be long before everyone knows the whole passage.

3. Hand out the 3″ x 5″ cards and the contracts.

4. As an incentive, announce that you'll all go on a bike ride or hike when everyone has learned his or her section. You may even want to add a trip to the ice cream shop for dessert.

5. Each person should fill out the contract, writing his or her name, the passage to be memorized, date, and signature.

6. Have family members sit in a circle and recite the passage, each saying his or her part in turn. Repeat until everyone has memorized the verse(s). Then see how many can say the *entire* passage by themselves.

7. Go out for your bike ride or hike. As you go, keep starting the recitation of the Scripture passage. The more you repeat it, the longer you all will retain it.

SUGGESTIONS:

I began this method of memorizing Scripture as much for *my* benefit as for my kid's. After years of having trouble keeping straight the list of the fruit of the Spirit, I finally committed it to memory in this manner: in my mind's eye, I pictured us taking turns around the table, each saying his section, like a "visual aid."

We've committed many verses to memory this way, and besides the obvious benefit of writing God's Word on our hearts, we've found that this particular system has bonding advantages also. By dividing the passage in this way we are dependent on one another and, as I shared earlier, we then memorize the entire section by picturing each other in our minds.

We use the contracts because they add a sense of commitment and importance to what we're doing. Signing our names in this manner somehow cements the idea that "I have agreed to do this and, therefore, I *will.*"

Later, we found the bike ride (or hike) to be so much fun—for the joy of just playing together and also because repeating the passage of Scripture set us apart as a special unit, a family connected in this unique commitment. Certainly the neighborhood will benefit too as you bike or march along proclaiming God's Word!

NATURE HIKE

MATERIALS NEEDED:
- [ ] Bible
- [ ] 3″ x 5″ file cards
- [ ] felt-tip pens (fine-tip) in assorted colors
- [ ] cardboard box and construction paper
- [ ] a nice day and a park or woods to hike in

TEXT: Philippians 4:8

PREPARATION:

[ ] On 3″ x 5″ cards, using colorful felt-tip markers, write out Philippians 4:8 as follows. (Words in italics should be emphasized with underlining or color.)
- (first card) "Finally, brothers, whatever is *true,* whatever is *noble,*
- (second card) whatever is *right,* whatever is *pure,*
- (third card) whatever is *lovely,* whatever is *admirable—*
- (fourth card) if anything is *excellent* or *praiseworthy—*think about such things."

This divides the qualities contained in the verses into equal amounts on each card.

[ ] Next, write one person's name on each card. (Each member of the family will be responsible for memorizing his or her card and also for finding something in nature that represents one or both of the qualities listed.) If you have more or fewer than four in your family, you will need to divide the verse differently. If possible, attempt to give each member of the family an equal number of qualities listed in the verses. Try to give Mom or Dad the first part of the verse so that a parent can start the recitation of the verse several times as you hike together.

[ ] Get cardboard box ready; decorate it with construction paper, if desired.

FAMILY TIME:

1. Announce that the family will be going on a nature hike, but first everyone must learn what special things in nature to look for.

2. Hand out 3″ x 5″ cards and have each person read his or her part aloud.

3. Keep repeating the process until everyone has memorized his or her part.

4. Go through the verse, asking your children what each quality means. For example, you may want to ask: **Just what does** *true* **mean? Can you think of a synonym? Can you think of an example of something that is true?** Do this for each quality.

5. Explain that everyone is to find something in nature that represents one quality (or each family may want to find something to represent *each* quality) on his or her card. You might need to give some ideas beforehand, especially for younger children. For example, say something like: *Noble* **means to be "great or magnificent to see." When you're outside, what seems to you to be very** *noble?* **How about the huge old oak in the park? Isn't it great and wonderful to look at, with its mighty arms reaching up to the heavens? To represent** *noble,* **you may want to find a branch or leaf from that grand tree.**

6. Continue to explain that, as you hike, each person will secretly put his find from nature in the box. You'll probably have to help by closing your eyes, but please do so. Keeping everyone's symbols from nature a secret is part of the fun for sharing later!

7. Go out to enjoy nature. Recite Philippians 4:8 (with a parent starting the verse several times), and collect your secret finds. You may need to help your children think of ideas (white flowers for *pure,* any flower for *lovely,* an intricate leaf for *praiseworthy,* etc.). Just make sure that everyone has slipped something into the box before you head home.

8. Later when you return home, have each person take a turn in the order of the verse and share what he or she found, what it represents, and why.

9. Finally, in prayer thank God for nature, His Word, and each other.

SUGGESTIONS:

I'll never forget the beautiful, crisp spring day when we went hiking through the woods of Tennessee, collecting our treasures. Finding symbols for these qualities seemed to bring the verses alive for us, and the boys found wonderful examples of *pure* (a dogwood branch in bloom) and *lovely* (a fragile spring flower) without any help or prompting from us. They thoroughly enjoyed the hike and then proudly shared their finds when we went home. We even were able to enjoy the flowers as a sweet reminder for several days afterward.

Again, this was a wonderful way to memorize God's Word, clearly explain what the qualities mean, and enjoy God's creation and each other. And certainly, we were doing *exactly* what the verse instructs us to do: *think on these things.*

BIBLE DRILLS

MATERIALS NEEDED:

- ☐ enough Bibles for each person in the family
- ☐ copies (enough for one per person) of several pages from your Bible's concordance (For example, you may want to copy the pages from your concordance that cite all the passages containing the word *love*.)
- ☐ 3″ x 5″ file cards
- ☐ felt-tip pens
- ☐ Scotch Tape

TEXT: Various

PREPARATION:

☐ Decide which entries from the concordance you wish to copy. You may choose to do several of God's characteristics—His love, justice, righteousness, truth, or purity. Then copy the pages from the concordance that contain these entries.

☐ Select one copy as the leader's answer key; choose which particular verses you will use for the Bible drills and underline these entries. (Again, you may wish to continue a theme, such as God's characteristics, and choose verses which speak of His love, righteousness, etc.)

☐ Construct a table marker, if desired, writing out one of the verses which you will later use.

FAMILY TIME:

1. Discuss the table marker verse during dinner. If you have chosen the theme of God's characteristics, be sure to use this time for teaching and discussion.

2. Have everyone put a Bible on his or her lap.

3. Hand out the copies of the concordances (probably one entry at a time, so that they don't get mixed up).

4. Explain the process: the leader will call out a phrase from the list in the concordance. For example, he may say, "The earth is full of His unfailing *love*." (Be sure everyone understands that the *l* in the entry substitutes for the word *love*.) Everyone must scan the

list under the word *love* to find the entry which matches this phrase (which will be found in Psalm 33:5). As soon as someone finds the phrase, he or she then must look up the verse in the Bible, stand up, and read the verse out loud. The leader should read the phrase over and over while the others search for the correct entry. Be sure to do enough so that (hopefully!) everyone wins at least once.

5. Close in prayer, thanking God for His love, justice, righteousness, etc.

SUGGESTIONS:

We've used Bible drills often—in all sorts of teaching situations: vacation Bible schools, Sunday School, Sunday evening workshops, and many times with our sons. When Craig came up with this variation on the drill, however, we realized that even more could be learned from this format. Too many times children feel awkward using a concordance, don't use one at all for this reason, or worse yet, don't even know it exists. By making the use of the concordance into a game, children quickly become familiar with its form (how letters stand for the word being noted) and also accustomed to looking up words and phrases. Of course, after finding the phrase, they also receive practice finding the book and verse in the Bible.

If your children are too young for this type of drill, you may want to simply tell which Bible verses to look up. And if your children vary a great deal in ages (and thus ability), you may need to adjust to make sure that all have an equal chance of finding the verse first. A few years ago, we would give our younger son a five-second head start. Now, we find no one needs any extra help—except maybe Mom and Dad, who can't keep up with their speedy sons.

Though the nature of the game makes this activity fairly competitive, stress constantly that the most important part is that we all are learning about God, His Word, and how to use His Word. Because of these goals, we are *all* winners!

BUILDING BLOCKS

MATERIALS NEEDED:
- ☐ Bible
- ☐ enough building blocks to make a replica of the temple
- ☐ a picture of the temple, from your Bible or another book (See list of helps at the end of this book.)
- ☐ paper and pencil for taking notes
- ☐ 3" x 5" file cards
- ☐ felt-tip pens
- ☐ Scotch Tape

TEXTS: Exodus 25; 1 Kings 6–7

PREPARATION:

☐ Construct the table marker, writing out 1 Kings 6:1: "In the four hundred and eightieth year after the Israelites had come out of Egypt, in the fourth year of Solomon's reign over Israel, in the month of Ziv, the second month, he began to build the _____." Leave out the last part about the temple so that you can build curiosity and interest by asking, "*What* did Solomon begin to build?" If your children know the answer, you can then begin discussing what the temple looked like.

☐ Study Exodus 25 and 1 Kings 6–7 so that you have a good idea of what the temple looked like and how to build it. Consult pictures in your Bible or other books to find a replica of the temple. In addition, see the Plan of Solomon's Temple on page 52.

☐ Test the building blocks that you will use to make sure that they will work well.

☐ You may wish to write out the main parts of the temple:
- Most holy place (containing the curtain covering its entrance, the ark of the covenant, and the cherubim guard)
- Holy place (which held 10 lampstands, 10 tables, and the altar of incense)
- Portico (inner courtyard)
- Outer courtyard (containing the sea of cast metal, the altar, and the movable stands of bronze)

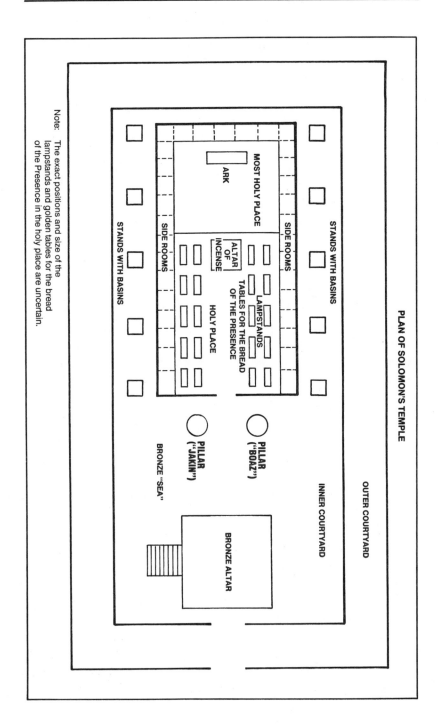

PLAN OF SOLOMON'S TEMPLE

Note: The exact positions and size of the lampstands and golden tables for the bread of the Presence in the holy place are uncertain.

☐ Do some research to discover the beautiful symbolism the temple shows. Your older children will enjoy this knowledge also.

FAMILY TIME:

1. At dinner, introduce the topic of the temple and begin discussing what it was like.

2. Read some parts of Exodus 25 and 1 Kings 6–7, or show the picture(s) of the temple. Explain how the different areas were used and why; describe them as best as you can. (Use as many pictures as you were able to find; the more you can show your children, the more they can picture in their minds.)

3. Build your own replica of the temple, allowing your children to do as much of the work as possible. Have them repeat to you what the parts of the temple are called, what they contained, and what they symbolized.

4. Close in prayer.

SUGGESTIONS:

If your children are really interested in building blocks and designing structures with them, this devotional should be one that they eagerly participate in. We found that both boys wanted to build the temple, and since they each had enough blocks to do so, we had *two* temples!

We also soon discovered that our older son had already studied the temple in some detail; thus, he was eager to share his knowledge with us and began quickly pointing out where different objects belonged. It was interesting for Craig and me to see him excitedly use what he had learned. Obviously, learning in a classroom was one thing; using his hands to put that knowledge to work in a touchable structure was another. As a teacher and a firm believer in visual aids, I believe that this type of visual aid—hands-on building—has the greatest potential for being remembered, and thus truly *learned,* for a long time.

Keep in mind too that this devotional easily adapts for older or younger children. If your children are older, give specifics and point out the beautiful symbolism of the temple objects. Younger children can still greatly enjoy building the walls of the temple and naming the objects inside. It seems that God has put an instinctive love of blocks and building (or crashing them?) into little ones. Watch for the signs that your children's interest is waning: when they want to begin bashing blocks, it's time to stop.

PROVERBS

MATERIALS NEEDED:
- [ ] Bible
- [ ] cookie sheet
- [ ] small bowl
- [ ] vinegar
- [ ] baking soda
- [ ] 3″ x 5″ file cards
- [ ] felt-tip marking pens
- [ ] pen
- [ ] Scotch Tape

TEXT: Proverbs 25:15-22 (The verse we will be concentrating on is verse 20.)

PREPARATION:

- [ ] Construct the table marker with felt-tip pens and pen, printing out all eight verses.

- [ ] Test your experiment. Place about two tablespoons of baking soda in the bowl. Set the bowl on the cookie sheet. Pour vinegar over the baking soda and watch it foam! (You may want to adjust the amount of baking soda for the effect that you desire.)

- [ ] Hide these materials so that you can keep this experiment a secret.

- [ ] Prepare to explain what a proverb is: *a wise saying given for instruction.* A biblical proverb often contains figurative language, and though it may be considered generally true, it will not *always* come true, for a proverb cannot be taken as a guarantee. However, the one who heeds its advice is wise. (You can find more information concerning proverbs in your Bible, or consult the list of helps at the back of this book for other sources of information.)

- [ ] You can come up with an additional example of the importance of paying close attention to the Book of Proverbs by considering the type of wise advice that your children will relate to. For example, you might ask your sports-crazed kid: **If so-and-so** (fill in the name of his or her current favorite sports hero) **told you that if you listened to this advice, you could make more**

shots (or catch more passes, kick more goals, etc.), **wouldn't you listen carefully? Wouldn't you try to do everything he or she told you? Especially because this person** *knows* **what he or she is talking about? Well, the same is true of the Bible's proverbs! A very wise and godly man (under the influence of the Holy Spirit) gave advice here in Proverbs for all kinds of situations, and we would be extremely wise to listen and do just what he says!**

You can adapt these questions for all types of interests that your children may have—a reader's favorite author ("If this author gave advice about how to write a good story . . ."), an artist, a computer lover, etc.

FAMILY TIME:

1. During dinner have family members (or just your children) take turns reading Proverbs 25:15-22.

2. Explain what a proverb is.

3. Give your examples of listening to a credible hero's advice; then link this to how and why the Proverbs can be so valuable to us.

4. Build interest and curiosity for tonight's devotion by stating emphatically: **We're going to actually test—with a scientific experiment—one of these verses! Can you guess which one it will be?** (Be sure to ask this with a twinkle in your eye and a slight grin!) Don't give anything away at this point; let them enjoy the suspense.

5. Take time, then, to discuss each verse and the wisdom that is given there. For example, stimulate conversation by saying something like: **Verse 1 is talking about how to convince a ruler or a leader over you to do something. Should you get impatient? Yell? What** *should* **you do? What about the captain of your soccer team? What could you do and say if you want to play a different position?** These proverbs are so clearly related to everyday life; make sure your children see that they touch their lives too.

6. After dinner, get out the soda, vinegar, bowl, and pan. Allow children to do the experiment themselves as much as possible. You may want to repeat it several times, giving each a turn at making a

mess! (What fun to make a mess on purpose!)

7. The last time you pour the vinegar over the soda, reread Proverbs 25:20, emphasizing what this action is being compared to. Discuss again what having a "heavy heart" means. Think of a specific example of someone you and your children know who is currently hurting. (You need not go into any specifics at this time.) Share how that person needs understanding and a concerned, listening ear, *not* someone who merely dismisses the hurt by saying, "Cheer up! Don't be sad! Life is great!" This type of "help" is no help at all and only makes more hurt feelings bubble out—like the vinegar does to the soda.

8. Conclude by praying for specific people who are hurting; then pray that each one of you will know how to give those people the type of help that they need, being sensitive to their feelings.

SUGGESTIONS:

This devotional moved from great fun (teasing the boys at the dinner table about which proverb we were going to do was hilarious) to interesting learning (we all benefited from the wise advice found in these verses) to sensitive concern for friends who were hurting (we all need the reminder to empathize and how important that is for true *ministering* to take place). Again, graphic visual aids are terrific tools for teaching children *and* adults, and this experiment teaches an unforgettable lesson.

Four
SELF-IMAGE

THUMBODY

MATERIALS NEEDED:
- ☐ Bible
- ☐ 3″ x 5″ cards, Scotch Tape, and felt-tip pens for table marker, if desired
- ☐ ink pad or broad felt-tip pens
- ☐ paper plates (Each member of the family will need one.)
- ☐ pencils or pens

TEXT: 1 Corinthians 12:12-26

PREPARATION:

☐ Read and study the Bible passage. The Corinthians mentioned in the passage were divided in opinion concerning gifts. Some thought that there were superior gifts, such as tongues; therefore, they envied or looked down on those with differing gifts. Paul makes the point here that *all* gifts are important and necessary. The uniqueness and diversity of the people—with their gifts—bring completeness to the body.

☐ Construct the table marker (printing verses on it).

☐ With felt-tip pens, write one family member's name at the top of each paper plate.

FAMILY TIME: Rd. The Little Engine that Could
1. Open with prayer.
2. Have one parent read 1 Corinthians 12:12-26. Explain what

was happening in the Corinthian church and then relate that our church today has the same differences among people which contribute to the completeness of the body of Christ.

3. To explain the analogy better, you may want to ask questions like:

- **Is any part of your body not important and needed?**
- **What if your little toe said, "I'm not important enough! I want to be a big toe!" What would you say?**
- **Why is each individual part necessary?**
- **Why can't every toe be a big toe? Could you walk that way?**

Make sure your children get the idea that each part is special, necessary, and cannot be what another part is—because that part is also important.

4. Looking at this principle in a different light, we can see that we bring special qualities into the family too. And just like in the church, each family member's unique contribution is needed to bring about unity and completeness. Make it very clear that we need each one of us; every member is somebody special.

5. Hand out paper plates. Discuss how God made each person with a unique thumbprint. Have everyone make a thumbprint in the center of his or her paper plate. (If you do not have an ink pad, you can make thumbprints by coloring the thumb with a felt-tip pen and then pressing it onto the plate.) Instruct everyone to write (just above the thumbprint): *"I am a thumbody because. . . ."*

6. Explain that you will pass the plates around to the other members of the family. Then each person should write something special that the "thumbprint owner" does for the family and especially for the person writing. Pass the plates around at least twice so that each person will have many comments on his or her plate.

7. Give plates back to their owners so they can enjoy reading what others have written.

8. Close in prayer, again thanking God for each member of the family.

SUGGESTIONS:

This was another of those devotionals that we did for the boys' benefit, and we parents ended up feeling very special! We all thoroughly enjoyed writing nice things about each other—noting along the way that each one did indeed contribute quite *different* things, but oh such *necessary* and *unique things!* The boys surprised us again by writing things that we hadn't expected (you mean he really does appreciate the help with homework?) and with the candor of their remarks ("loves me when I'm in a pickle!"). And it was also helpful for Craig and me to point out the specific ways our children contribute to our home—that they are truly as needed as parents.

These plates were so special to each one of us that we then posted them on the doors of our rooms. When we moved to a new house, the plates were taped carefully onto the new doors. And whenever I need a lift or encouragement as a mom, I head right for my paper plate; it has miraculous healing powers!

One final note: we also included our much-loved (and spoiled) dog in this one. Yes, we made a plate (complete with fake paw print in the center) for him too and wrote reasons why he also is "thumbody" in our home. The boys thoroughly enjoyed this and made sure that Bojangles had his paper plate posted above his rug in the kitchen.

- Games
- Ice cream bars

CLAY "MONSTERS"

MATERIALS NEEDED:
- [ ] Bible
- [ ] Play-Doh or clay—enough for each member of the family to construct a small creature (different colors, if possible)
- [ ] magazines with pictures of all different types of adults and children
- [ ] a separate picture of each member of the family
- [ ] a manila folder or small sack
- [ ] 3" x 5" file cards
- [ ] felt-tip pens (broad- and fine-tip)
- [ ] Scotch Tape

TEXT: Psalm 139:1-14

PREPARATION:
- [ ] Read and study Psalm 139.
- [ ] Construct the table marker, writing out Psalm 139:1-14. Bend three file cards in half; this should allow them to stand up. Write "nice" on one card, "OK" on the second, and "nobody" on the third.
- [ ] Make a fourth card that boldly says "*SOMEBODY* in God's eyes!" (Fold this card also.)
- [ ] Cut out pictures of adults and children. Be sure to get a wide assortment of people—clean and dirty, white- and blue-collar workers, elegant and plain, and all different races. Try to get at least 20 pictures.
- [ ] Put all the pictures in a pile, including the pictures of your family. Mix them up and place in the manila folder or sack.

FAMILY TIME:

1. At dinner, have your children take turns reading the verses from Psalm 139:1-14.

2. To stimulate discussion, you may want to ask questions like:

- **In what different ways does God know us?** (our movements, thoughts, comings and goings, our ways and habits, where we are even in darkness)

- **Is there anywhere we can go where God is not?** (You may want to list places and times that your children fear.)
- **Who made us? When? How does the psalmist describe us?** (fearfully and wonderfully made)
- **How does it make you feel to know that God's Word says that His works are wonderful, and *we* are His work?**

3. Later, hand out the Play-Doh. (Give everyone different colors, if possible.) Tell everyone to make the ugliest monster possible. Allow plenty of time to enjoy the pleasure of being creative.

4. After you've finished with the monsters, place the three cards (nice, OK, and nobody) so that you can pile your pictures underneath.

5. Take the pictures out of the folder and ask for each one: **Which pile does *this* person belong in—nice, OK, or nobody?** Try not to put any indication of placement in your voice or actions; let your children decide where they go. (Hopefully you'll have some in each pile so that you can make a point later!)

6. When you've gone through the pictures, decide which pile your monsters belong in. This way you should be sure to have some "nobodies".

7. Reread Psalm 139:13-14 and ask: **What conditions does God put on being wonderfully made? In other words, does it say that only the beautiful people are wonderfully made? Those with nice clothes? Those making lots of money? The non-handicapped? Those of a certain skin color?** Once your children understand the line of reasoning, allow them to come up with as many different "nonconditions" as they can. Reinforce in many ways that God loves all of us just as we are, and that each one of us is "wonderfully made" in His eyes no matter what people of this world think or say. Also emphasize that if God says this, we should think this same way about ourselves and others.

8. Announce that now family members will go through the pile of people again, putting them where God says they should be. Place the fourth card out (*"SOMEBODY* in God's eyes") and go through each picture again, reinforcing that yes, this one and that one (through the entire stack) is indeed *somebody.* Lastly, even a monster is a somebody!

9. Close in prayer, asking God to help us see each person He has

made as His creation—and therefore, *wonderful.*

SUGGESTIONS:

Craig and I have constantly hammered home the idea that God loves us for who we are *inside,* not for what we look like outside. But still, offhand comments here and there plus the unending bombardment by the media (that we must all be shipshape, beautiful, rich, talented, and smart too) encourage incorrect judgments of worth to seep in. For example, pictures of workers who were really dirty (you know the ones—from those laundry detergent ads!) caused our boys to exclaim, "Oh, gross! He sure looks like a nobody!" And we had been afraid that the devotion might not work because they'd put *everyone* in the "nice" pile.

In retrospect, I believe this devotional time was good for children *and* parents, for we could first reemphasize that everyone—no matter what—is somebody in God's eyes. And second, while we again recognized the need to contradict whatever wrong concepts television may have presented, Craig and I were reminded that we can't always blame that one-eyed monster. *We* also need to watch our comments concerning others' appearances.

SECRET PALS

MATERIALS NEEDED:
- [ ] a Bible for each member of the family
- [ ] 3" x 5" file cards
- [ ] felt-tip pens
- [ ] Scotch Tape

TEXTS: Ephesians 6:18-20; 2 Thessalonians 1:11-12; James 5:13-16

PREPARATION:

[ ] Construct table markers which say, "Secret Pals are great!" and "Secret Pal????" or any other sayings you may want to use to create curiosity.

[ ] Look up and read the Scripture verses listed above. Decide how to divide the verses so that everyone has a section to read. Print these sections of verses and names on file cards which will be handed out later.

[ ] Have blank cards and felt-tip pens ready for later use.

[ ] Think through activities that you can suggest that your children do for their Secret Pals. These are some of the things that we have done:

- Leave frequent notes on the Secret Pal's desk or dresser that say things like, "I'm praying for you!" or "I love you, Secret Pal! Signed, ?"
- Secretly slip a note of encouragement into the Secret Pal's packed lunch (for work or school).
- Buy a treat such as a candy bar and sneak it into the Secret Pal's room.
- Either purchase or make a card for the Secret Pal. Many card stores have cards specifically for Secret Pals.
- Do something helpful (secretly, of course!) for the Secret Pal, such as make his or her bed or do one of his or her chores. A child could do one of his or her *own* chores without any nagging reminders from Mom or Dad. (What a gift!)
- Compose a poem for the Secret Pal.
- Color a special picture for the Secret Pal. (This one is especially good for the little ones as they all can do this.)

- Purchase some little item that the Secret Pal would enjoy (such as a bookmark, pencil, eraser, or any other small object from a Christian bookstore).
- And most important, remind family members to *pray* for their Secret Pals!

FAMILY TIME:

1. During dinner, talk about the idea of having Secret Pals. You may want to use the example of David and Jonathan from 1 Samuel 18:1-4 and 1 Samuel 20. In these passages, David and Jonathan make a covenant between them, pledging to love and protect each other. By Jonathan's statements throughout chapter 20 (in v. 13, "May the Lord be with you"), we can assume that they did indeed pray for each other also.

2. Begin the family devotional by opening with prayer.

3. Hand out everyone's Bible and card with assigned verses to read.

4. Take turns reading and then ask: **What theme is in all of these verses?**

Then, teach them the mechanics of praying for one another by asking questions such as:

- **How often should we pray for others?** (all occasions, constantly; explain that means set-aside times *and* whenever we think of others)
- **What should we pray for one another?** (all kinds of things: that Christ may be glorified in us; for help with troubles, unhappiness, sickness, and sins that we need to confess and correct)
- **How can we know specifically what to pray for one another?** (by sharing ourselves and asking each other for needs)

5. With parents setting an example first, begin sharing prayer requests with each other.

6. Explain that you will draw names for Secret Pals and that these pals will be responsible to pray for each other this week. List your other suggestions of surprises for Secret Pals also.

7. Each one should write his or her name on a card, fold it, put it in the pile, and draw the name of another person.

8. Close in prayer.

SUGGESTIONS:

We've used this devotional many times, and yet if it has been a while since we've exchanged names, our kids will ask, "Isn't it about time for Secret Pals again?" Obviously, they enjoy this activity very much, and not just the receiving side. As a matter of fact, I believe their favorite part is the sneaking around, leaving cute notes and surprises. And this can do wonders for a family that has been a bit on the edgy side.

Parents, just make sure that you do not forget to do those notes, helpful actions, and surprises. Once children catch on to the joy of this "giving," their participation just may put us adults to shame!

Five
WORSHIP

CONSECRATION

MATERIALS NEEDED:
- [ ] Bible
- [ ] large candle (possibly your wedding candle)
- [ ] enough medium-sized rocks for each member of the family, plus a couple more
- [ ] matches
- [ ] 3″ x 5″ cards
- [ ] felt-tip pen
- [ ] tape

TEXT: Joshua 4:1-9

PREPARATION:
- [ ] Collect rocks (hand-sized is nice), and put them in a pile. (I suggest more than needed to avoid possible conflict!)
- [ ] Have candle and matches ready.
- [ ] Construct the table marker. Use Joshua 4:6 *or* draw an altar of stones (see p. 70) and write, "What do these stones mean?"
- [ ] Read and study Joshua 4:1-9.
- [ ] This devotional is more effective when it is dark outside; thus, you may want to do this at a later hour.

FAMILY TIME:
1. During dinner, introduce the topic and build curiosity by asking questions such as:

69

- **What do *you* think these stones stand for?**
- **Why do you think Israel made a pile of rocks like this?**
- **Can you remember other times in the Bible when people built an altar?**

2. Open the devotional time with prayer.

3. Read Joshua 4:1-9 aloud. Discuss the background—how God had taken the Israelites out of Egypt and through the wilderness, and then was leading them into the Promised Land. Emphasize the hope and excitement the Israelites must have felt, as well as the fear of an unknown land.

4. Make sure that your children sense the awe and worship of God that the Israelites experienced as they built this significant altar, and how it would always be a reminder of their great God and what He had done for them. Ask: **What do you think the Israelites' children would want to know when they saw this altar? What would their parents tell them, do you think?**

5. Have each family member choose a rock.

6. Light the candle and turn off other lights.

7. As everyone holds his or her rock, discuss how faith is even more real and firmer than the rock.

8. Ask everyone to give prayer requests. Conclude by praying for each other.

SUGGESTIONS:

Because this devotion calls for application of principles, do not attempt this with young children (ages seven or eight and under). Small ones are not yet ready for comprehending the seriousness of this worship time.

We developed this family altar when our world suddenly turned upside down: due to serious financial problems at Craig's place of work, he was released. I was struggling with this when I realized that I needed to work this out with my Lord, not only for my sake but also for the boys'. I knew without a doubt that I would be a visible testimony that faith works not only in good times but *especially* during the bad. For this reason it was important to us that our boys experience this tough time *with* us. Rather than shielding them from what was happening (keeping all circumstances secret), we desired that they see faith at work in our lives. (Please note, however, that we did not "bare our souls" to our children. We need to use judgment in what and how much is appropriate to tell our kids. *Never* should parents burden their children with too much emotional baggage.)

The focus of our sharing was the uncertainty and insecurity we felt at this time. We stressed, however, that we knew our faith was based on the God who is more real and solid than the rocks which we now held in our hands. We emphasized that no matter what the circumstances were, we also knew God would take care of us. (This emphasis was probably as much for our benefit as the boys'.) Our altar, then, became a consecration of ourselves to dependence and belief in our Lord. We would trust Him no matter what, and we agreed to light the candle each evening until we knew where God was sending us.

This was an emotional, stirring, and heart-warming devotion for our family. We bonded in our need for each other, and I felt more secure knowing that we all were as one in our united commitment to His will at this time.

God *did* miraculously provide another ministry for us, and our sons (and Craig and I too) did indeed observe faith work in difficult times. We learned much about faith because of this experience, and we also learned that there is strength in the unique and special bonding a family can provide.

DEDICATION

MATERIALS NEEDED:
- ☐ Bible
- ☐ 3″ x 5″ file cards
- ☐ felt-tip pens (fine-tip)
- ☐ Scotch Tape
- ☐ large candle
- ☐ enough smaller candles for each member of the family
- ☐ matches

TEXT: Hebrews 13:20-21

PREPARATION:

☐ This devotion is designed to be used when you have made a major purchase—such as a home, car, piano, etc.—and you wish to dedicate the object to the Lord's use.

☐ Construct the table marker, writing out Hebrews 13:20-21; underline or highlight in color the words "for doing His will."

☐ Have candles and matches ready for later. You may wish to put the large candle in the center of your dining room table, with the smaller candles around it.

☐ Think through specific ways in which you as a parent intend to use this purchase to serve God; then think of possible suggestions for your children. For example, if you have bought a new home, you may plan to serve visiting missionaries a special meal or entertain unsaved neighbors. If you have purchased a new car, you might decide to use it to deliver meals to the elderly or to visit lonely ones in a nursing home. Children also can invite over unsaved friends or go with you to a nursing home. A new piano can be used to offer up music as worship to God, and a new dining room set can be recognized as a place where you will entertain God's people. Be prepared with several uses for the purchase in case your children cannot think of any later.

FAMILY TIME:

1. At the dinner table have your children read the verses on the table marker.

2. Begin a discussion of why God graciously gives us so many things. Draw the answer out of your children by asking:

- **According to these verses, does God give us things to use only for ourselves?**
- **Does God give us things to protect selfishly, so they don't get messed up?**
- **Does God give us things to share grudgingly with others?**
- **Does God gives us things to share, then, because that makes us feel good? No? Then why?**

Make sure that they understand that *everything* God gives us is to use to do His will. Then discuss how we do His will—by worshiping Him, by maturing in Him ourselves (through reading His Word and prayer) and then edifying others, by witnessing to others, and glorifying Him in everything we do.

3. After dinner gather around the big candle at the table and light it, turning other lights out if possible. Give each member of the family his or her candle to hold.

4. Announce that you are having this devotion to dedicate the newly purchased item to God. Even though you recognize that everything belongs to Him anyway, this is a way you can remind yourselves anew that this object also belongs to God.

5. Remind family members that every good gift is for "doing His will." Therefore, each one should think of one way that this new object will be used by him or her to do His will. Give everyone a few moments to think; you may want to sing the chorus "God Is So Good" a couple of times.

6. As each person shares a response, he or she should light a candle. (You may need to offer your suggestions at this point.)

7. Close in prayer there at the table, or if you wish, move to the object which you are dedicating. You may also choose to do your dedication prayer on your knees. Make sure that your prayer again recognizes that this object belongs to God, and that your desire is to use it to serve Him.

SUGGESTIONS:

This worship time has become so much a part of our family life that I think we would feel empty—as if something so important had been left out—if we did not dedicate each major purchase to God. And who is to decide what is major and what is not? If a child considers a new clarinet, a bike, or a computer to be of major significance, then why not dedicate these also?

You may be pleasantly surprised by the perceptive answers your children think of for how they will use these purchases to serve God. I've also noticed a definite lessening of the this-is-mine-so-don't-hurt-it attitude concerning the objects we dedicated. When there has been a very definite "setting apart" for Him—whether the new object gets messed up from use or not—we all seem to have a better hold on priorities.

When we bought our new car, we also gave it a name—Samuel (Sammy for short)—because like Hannah, we cried out our need to God and He answered our prayers! Now, every time we speak of Sammy we are subconsciously reminded of God's goodness to us in providing for our needs. And that's a great reminder for Mom too: whether it works well or breaks down, it's still God's car, to do with as He sees fit.

SENTENCE PRAYERS

MATERIALS NEEDED:
- ☐ Bible
- ☐ 3″ x 5″ file cards
- ☐ felt-tip pens (fine-tip)
- ☐ Scotch Tape
- ☐ several sheets of paper

TEXT: Philippians 4:6-7

PREPARATION:

☐ Construct the table marker, printing out Philippians 4:6-7.

☐ Have paper and a marker set aside for later.

☐ Think through some concerns which may be troubling your children at the present time. These should be things which they will feel comfortable talking about at the dinner table. Consider how your children might be comforted through discussion and prayer about these concerns.

☐ For the prayertime think of prayer requests for others which will be relevant to your children.

FAMILY TIME:

1. At dinner, read the verses on the table marker.

2. Announce that family members are soon going to learn a new way to pray, but first you want to talk about things which family members might be concerned about. Point out that talking to God can help us feel at peace concerning these kinds of problems.

3. Gently begin asking questions about those areas of concern in your children's lives. (For example, if the playground has become a major source of consternation for a child, you may want to ask:

- **How are things going on the playground these days? Is someone playing with you?**
- **Are the children playing fairly?**
- **If not, how does this make you feel when it happens?**
Your child may reply by saying "lonely" or "very angry." Encourage him or her by assurances that Jesus understands and cares about us; He is always with us, loving us.)

4. Remind them that they can pray to God anywhere, anytime, and that He always hears them—even a very quick prayer.

5. Later, sit around the table with the paper and felt-tip pen in the middle.

6. Ask them to list every request that they can think of for themselves and others. As they are listed, one person should write each request on the sheet of paper.

7. Again remind everyone of the assurance that God gave us in Philippians 4:6-7—that He gives peace to those who are troubled when we offer those requests with thanksgiving to Him.

8. Explain that family members will pray "sentence prayers," which means that as you take turns praying, each person says only one or two sentences at a time for these requests. You can then proceed in whichever way is best for your family: simply go down the list, each person praying in turn; *or* you may want to assign specific requests to certain people. If you do this, be sure to put the names by the requests so that you do not forget any.

9. Continue down the list until you have prayed for each one. Have one family member say a final, closing "thank-You" to God.

SUGGESTIONS:

If any of your children are uncomfortable about praying out loud, this devotion can be a great encourager. One might easily feel threatened and uneasy about saying long prayers, but a quick sentence is much less intimidating. Eventually these sentence prayers may become stepping-stones to a more mature prayer life.

It's funny too how children may not like to say very much at one time. One very long prayer is probably unusual for elementary-aged children. (Toddlers are another matter—"and thank You for Kitty and Spot and grass and sky. . . ."–especially at the end of the day when Mom and Dad are dead tired.) Yet when we break up the prayer into several different ones, taking turns, children will end up praying a very long prayer. Don't make the mistake of telling them this, though; it must remain a parental secret!

Often now our children will request to do sentence prayers. They enjoy listing all their many concerns, and they enjoy praying for others too. It has become a very natural process for them, and that is a tremendous leap up those stepping-stones.

PREPARING FOR SUNDAY

MATERIALS NEEDED:
- ☐ Bible
- ☐ 3″ x 5″ file cards
- ☐ felt-tip pens
- ☐ Scotch Tape
- ☐ resources with pictures, if possible
- ☐ dictionary

TEXT: Find out which text your pastor will be using the next Sunday.

PREPARATION:

☐ Construct the table marker, printing out the verses your pastor will be using. If the text is too long, print out a portion of the verses.

☐ Write "bless" on one 3″ x 5″ card, "teach" on another, and "convict" on a third card.

☐ Consult your Bible or another resource for background on the Scripture passage. For example, you will want to find out to whom this was written (the people of what town or country, and whether they were Jews, Gentiles, or a mixture of both); approximately when it was written (in relation to major events plus the date); and possibly the historical climate at that time (political events and any other information pertinent to this section of Scripture). You will find a list of suggested resources at the end of this book. Those with pictures would be of special interest to your children.

☐ Have the dictionary on hand for later use. You may want to use one dictionary per child if possible.

FAMILY TIME:

1. Have your children read the Scripture on the table marker; explain the background of this passage to them. You may wish to briefly discuss the verses also.

2. Later, open your devotion time with prayer.

3. Hand out the three cards to your children—one per child or

double up as necessary. Tell them to look up these words in the dictionary and write down their meanings on the cards.

4. When all are finished, have them read the meanings out loud. To reinforce the understanding, ask them to then give the definitions in their own words.

5. Explain that to be blessed, taught, and convicted are the main responses we experience as Christians to God's Word. You will want to amplify this further by asking questions for each response:

- *Blessed*—**What does it feel like to be blessed?** (warm, happy, tingly inside, joyful, loved) **What can a blessing motivate us to do?** (worship God, seek Him more, praise God)
- *Taught*—**What does it feel like when you are listening to God's Word and you learn something brand-new?** (exciting, interesting, curious to learn more) **What can this motivate us to do?** (read to learn more, try to *do* what we've learned, tell others what we've learned)
- *Convicted*—**What does it feel like when you feel conviction or sorrow for sin?** (sad, humble, ashamed, unworthy) **What should this motivate us to do?** (seek repentance, pray, change our behavior, accept His forgiveness)

6. Explain that on Sunday family members should have at least one response to the pastor's sermon, and possibly two or all three. Ask everyone to listen carefully so that during Sunday dinner you can tell each other what your responses were, how you felt, and what you are motivated to do.

7. Close in prayer, asking that the Holy Spirit would help each one understand whatever special message He has for each family member on Sunday.

SUGGESTIONS:

This devotion is intended for older elementary children since younger ones may be in children's church or too little to comprehend or begin to listen to the pastor's sermon.

When your children are old enough to sit in church and yet too old to draw pictures or stare into the ozone, you may want to try this. For many years now I have prayed that the Holy Spirit would bless, teach, or convict me before I begin to read the Bible for my personal devotions. Since it had proved to be effective for me, I decided to adopt the same pattern for the boys for Sunday morning. (I have also taught them to do this for their personal devotions too.) We found that it did help quite a bit, and it helped us parents to concentrate better too. Our dinner conversations are often quite interesting and revealing, and I'm always amazed at what children can pick up when they are motivated to do so.

A friend of ours suggested also that we try having the boys draw a picture that represented what the pastor was saying. Again, they often amazed us with their perception and understanding. Maybe every pew should provide blank paper and crayons!

CHURCH AT HOME

MATERIALS NEEDED:
- [ ] Bible
- [ ] some type of table for a pulpit
- [ ] a hymnbook, if possible
- [ ] paper and pen for the "Order of Service"
- [ ] instruments—piano, trombone, French horn, whatever your children can play.

TEXT: Choose an exciting story such as Judges 6–7 (the suspenseful and triumphant story of Gideon); Judges 4–5 (the account of Deborah—a prophetess—and especially of interest to girls); or Judges 14–16 (many lessons to be learned from Samson).

PREPARATION:

- [ ] First of all, you need a huge amount of snow—or any other inclement weather conditions—since this devotion should be done on a Sunday when you must miss church! You may also want to do this if a family member is ill or if you have overnight visitors who are not comfortable attending church, but *will* "attend" in your home.

- [ ] Select the Scripture story that you wish to use. Have a parent or older sibling study the passage. That person should prepare to tell the story with as much excitement and suspense as possible. (A list of resources can be found at the end of this book.)

- [ ] Tell your children that you will be having a very special church service there at home. Assign them the task of preparing the music, choosing the songs they wish to sing and special instrumental music. Encourage one or more to volunteer to play an instrument. Have them write out an "Order of Service."

- [ ] Arrange your living room or family room for your worship service. Place a pulpit or podium of some sort (if desired), arrange couch and chairs, and have instruments ready.

FAMILY TIME:

1. Call to worship and opening prayer.
2. Follow the "Order of Service" given by your children. (They

may have several songs and special music at this point.) If one of your children is willing, have him or her lead the singing just like at church.

3. The designated speaker should preach the sermon with excitement and suspense. (No sleepers during *this* sermon!) If possible, use pictures or any other visual aids to add to the story.

4. Sing one or two additional songs at this point. Repeat earlier selections if others have not been chosen.

5. Close in prayer.

SUGGESTIONS:

The first time we participated in church at home, everyone was already excited since the service had been cancelled because of snow. (This was in Tennessee, and measurable amounts of snow where we lived were very rare.) The boys responded eagerly, adding their own creative touches to a service that we all knew would be an imitation—and yet fun in its uniqueness.

It has been interesting to see their responses to all the different parts of a worship service: since both boys are musical, they have been eager to lead singing and play instruments. One time they even printed bulletins and handed them out stoically as Craig and I came through the family room door for church!

Somehow this worship time gives us a feeling of coziness, belonging, and completeness in being *just us.* You notice in your children's eyes (maybe for the first time) that they realize that church isn't really a building. Instead they see before them that church is people—people worshiping Almighty God. And even more important, they know that church is parents and children—brother, sister, and *me*—worshiping God.

Six
USING MUSIC

MUSIC PRAISE NIGHT

MATERIALS NEEDED:

☐ Bible
☐ 3″ x 5″ file cards
☐ felt-tip pens
☐ any sort of junk that has creative possibilities: paper towel tubes, plastic fruit baskets, yarn, ribbon, paper plates, small boxes, straws, spoons, Popsicle sticks, etc.
☐ Scotch Tape and masking tape
☐ glue

TEXT: Psalm 95:1-3

PREPARATION:

☐ Collect all your junk and put it in a large box or sack.
☐ Construct the table marker, writing out Psalm 95:1-3 on both sides.

☐ Later you will be creating "instruments of praise" (with your assorted junk); therefore, you need to think up names for these instruments. Each member will choose the name that he or she likes best and then construct the music maker. To avoid any possible arguments over these names, I suggest that you think up at least one more than the number of people in your family. For example, since we have four in our family, I had five names, which were: Williford's *Woozleum,* Williford's *Whazoo,* Williford's *Wump-thumper,* Williford's *Whirlygiggy,* and Williford's *Wham-*

bammer! Try to use this first-letter alliteration with your last name and attempt to make the instruments' names sound different also. Note how Whambammer sounds like a type of drum; Whazoo, a horn. Heaven knows what a Woozleum is!

☐ Write your creative instrument names on the file cards using different colors of felt-tip pens.

☐ Think of a few choruses that everyone in your family knows. You may want to consider "Praise Him, Praise Him, All You Little Children" or "Allelu, Allelu, Allelu, Allelujah! Praise Ye the Lord!"

FAMILY TIME:

1. At dinner, have your children read the verses on the table marker. Discuss the actions and responses associated with singing to our God. For example, you may want to ask:

➤ **What feelings do these verses mention?** (joy, thankfulness)

➤ **What actions and motivations do we bring to God?** (with joy, shouting joyfully, with thanksgiving, with psalms, recognizing Him as the Rock and the great God!)

➤ **What should our response be to our singing?** (praise as we know His wonderful salvation and see His greatness)

Be sure that you get across the idea that singing or playing music before God is *not* a passive thing; we need to worship Him actively with our whole hearts. And emphasize especially the aspect of *joy*, for singing and playing to God is fun!

2. Later, bring out your creative junk.

3. Announce that you will be making instruments of praise— *whatever* each one chooses to create out of all these supplies. You may want to say something like: **These instruments already have names; they are just waiting for each of you to put them together so we'll know what they look like!** Then, call out the names and allow family members to choose which one he or she wishes to create. Allow plenty of time for everyone to tape, glue, construct, and test his or her instrument.

4. When all are finished, announce that you will now sing and shout joyfully to God in song and with instruments. (Those who need to blow air into their instruments will not be able to sing, obviously!) Sing and play your selected choruses, praising God

together. Your children may want to choose other songs to sing or play also.

5. Close in prayer, thanking God for the joy we experience as we worship Him with music.

SUGGESTIONS:

If anyone could have seen—or heard—us on the night that we did this, we would never have been asked to sing in a choir or do special music again. But fortunately, just the Willifords' band was present, so we sang, and played, and created a huge racket until our dog looked at us like we were crazy.

Very little ones can join in for this devotional, though they may need some encouragement and help putting together an instrument. The reality of joyful worship through music comes alive for children when they know the songs and can participate in singing them. Just be sure, parents, that whatever sounds end up coming out of these creations (and there probably will be some strange and *loud* ones), you must convey joy! And aren't we glad that God accepts even off-key and slightly different musical praise?

EVALUATING MUSIC

MATERIALS NEEDED:
- ☐ Bible
- ☐ 3″ x 5″ file cards
- ☐ felt-tip pens (fine-tip)
- ☐ Scotch Tape
- ☐ plain, notebook-sized paper
- ☐ pens or pencils
- ☐ at least 10 records or tapes of differing music; I would suggest one from each of these categories:
  - • Christian contemporary—group and single
  - • Christian rock—group and single
  - • classical (instrumental)
  - • secular easy-listening
  - • secular hard rock (NOTE: *not* something containing satanic references, sexual references, swearing, etc., as I would not bring this into my home)
  - • secular "lite" rock
  - • any others you may desire to use
- ☐ access to a copying machine, if possible

TEXTS: Psalm 98:4-6; Ephesians 5:19-20

PREPARATION:

☐ Construct the table marker, writing out the verses from Psalm 98 on one side and the Ephesians verses on the other.

☐ Choose several recording artists of differing styles; the more varieties you can put together, the better. For example, we chose to use two songs by a Christian contemporary single—one soft rock and one more easy-listening. We also chose two by a secular rock group, but one was hard rock and one, slow and melodic. The classical piece I chose was "Mars" from *The Planets* by Holst; it has a driving rock beat!

☐ Write out the "Music Night" rating sheet, then make enough copies for each member of the family to have one, plus one extra. Use a black felt-tip pen to print a sheet that looks something like this:

MUSIC NIGHT

Rate each on a scale of 1 (poor) to 8 (excellent).

ARTIST(S)	WORDS	MELODY	MY RESPONSE	TESTIMONY	OVERALL
1.					
2.					
3.					

List all the music you will evaluate. For example we decided to use ten recording artists.

Leave enough room on the sheet for the evaluator to put his or her rating responses.

Gather your selected records and tapes; have them ready and in order for later. You will probably need to make a list and note which song on the album or tape you have selected.

FAMILY TIME:

1. At dinner, take turns reading the verses on the table marker.

2. Discuss the reasons that we make music: for joy, with jubilance, to edify one another (Eph. 5:19), to sing in our hearts, to give thanks for everything. You may also want to ask: **What types of instruments and music are listed here?** (harp, trumpet, and ram's horn; psalms, hymns, and spiritual songs) Point out that these are quite different, and yet they all have one purpose: to praise God.

3. Later, move to your tape player, stereo, or CD player and explain that you will be listening to several different types of music. Each person will rate the selections on a scale of one to eight, with one being rated "poor" and eight considered "excellent." Explain what each category means:

- *Words*—the meaning of the lyrics, whether you like them or not. (Instrumentals will obviously not be rated for words.)
- *Melody*—rate whether the piece has a melody or not and if you like it.
- *My response*—rate your feelings about the words and melody.

- *Testimony*—this grades the performer's appearance, lifestyle (as best as you can perceive).
- *Overall*—the entire effect of this selection on you.

4. Ask for questions about this activity. When they have been answered, proceed through the music selections, giving everyone time to fill out the sheet before beginning the next song. (NOTE: sometimes you may not want to listen to the entire song if your point has already been made!)

5. When you have finished all the songs, compare ratings and discuss your differences. Be sensitive to personal preferences, and yet try to come to some conclusions concerning the importance of personal testimony of the performer and what the lyrics are saying. Most important, point out that *all* music needs to be carefully evaluated in these main areas to judge if it truly is praising God as directed in Ephesians 5 and Psalm 98.

SUGGESTIONS:

Because one son was entering the teen years and because we'd heard comments on the order of, *"All* music like that is bad," we wanted to ensure that our sons had a way to evaluate music—*on their own.* We did not want them to simply accept or reject music on our recommendation, for this doesn't provide a tool for independent discernment as they grow older. And I think that is the key element that Craig and I were striving for in this devotion—discernment. For if we have taught a child to discern we have given that child more than a one-time gift; we've given him a reusable and essential tool for the future.

BUILDING AN ARK

MATERIALS NEEDED:

- [ ] tape or record of the song "Build an Ark" (We used a tape by the New Gaither Vocal Band entitled *New Point of View,* Word, Inc., 1984.)
- [ ] tape recorder or record player
- [ ] construction paper
- [ ] felt-tip pens (broad- and fine-tip)
- [ ] 3″ x 5″ file cards
- [ ] Scotch Tape

TEXT: Genesis 6–9

PREPARATION:

- [ ] Read the Scripture text—the account of Noah and the ark. Study briefly.
- [ ] Construct the table marker, drawing a small ark on each side. You may wish to color it also.
- [ ] Draw a large picture of the ark on construction paper, or photocopy the picture on page 90. Leave plenty of room to print phrases on the area surrounding the ark. Just draw an outline of the ark, leaving the inside uncolored.
- [ ] Listen to the song, "Build an Ark," a couple of times; have it ready to play later.
- [ ] Think through any problems occurring outside the home that your children may be struggling with: playground bullies, teasing from schoolmates, fighting on the bus, getting along with neighborhood children, etc. Be ready to give these as suggestions during the devotion if your children do not respond to the question, "What problems are you experiencing outside our 'ark'—our home?"
- [ ] Have your picture of the large ark and fine-tip markers ready for use later.

FAMILY TIME:

1. During dinner indicate the table marker and ask: **What is this a picture of?** Then, encourage your children to tell the story of

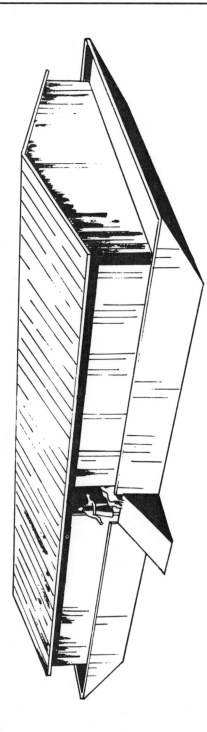

Noah. Supply any details of the story which they leave out. Be sure to emphasize God's involvement—His instructions, protection, and care.

2. To build interest, announce: **Our family has built a type of ark. Did you know that? Later during devotions we'll talk about** *our* **ark!"**

3. Later, have family members gather around the record/tape/CD player. Ask everyone to listen carefully and then play the song "Build an Ark."

4. In your own words tell your family something like this: **Our family is an ark too! God has been very much a part of our marriage and then your birth(s). He has given us instructions about how to protect you and how to raise you in His ways. Outside of our "safe ark," though, there is a storm of problems that we as parents can't always protect you from. What are some of the problems that you are experiencing outside of our home?**(Give suggestions, if necessary.)

As children—and parents too—list problems, write them on the picture *outside* of the ark. When everyone has listed at least two, write family members' names on the *inside* of the ark. Emphasize that God is here with us in our "ark," but He is also with us wherever we go.

5. Encourage your children by reminding them again that although these problems do exist outside of your home, your "ark" will be a place of safety, a place where you as a family will love and support each other (parents supporting children *and* children supporting parents *and* children supporting children)—always.

6. Listen to "Build an Ark" once again.

7. As you sit and hold hands in a circle, pray for each other. You may want to assign names.

SUGGESTIONS:

When I think of all the potentially hurtful situations that wait to "gobble up" our boys when each steps one foot out the door, I get very anxious. (My mind envisions this huge monster with its mouth open, waiting!) And as a parent I often feel so helpless to protect our children; other times I realize that they need these troubling experiences for God to mold them into the men they will one day be. I do want our guys to know, however, that our home will always be a place of security, love, and support. No matter what they may need to face "out there," here at home they will find love.

This devotional has been a constant reminder to me to make sure our family members support each other. Whenever the boys have called each other names, they have heard me repeat many times, "No! In this house we do not tear each other down. You may have to listen to that at school, but we do not tolerate that here." Again, we're emphasizing that we build up each other in our family's ark.

We used this song because it had long been a favorite of our sons and also because it symbolically presented the concept that we wanted to teach so well. If your family has a favorite song that has helpful words, just use a format similar to this devotion to adapt that song to fit your needs. Music can be a powerful teaching tool, and children generally listen and relate well if the music is within their conceptual capabilities. One more benefit—we found that a lesson learned through music is not easily forgotten: we hummed "Build an Ark" for days!

Seven
AIMING FOR TROUBLE SPOTS

SPORTSMANSHIP: GOOD SPORTS VS. BAD SPORTS

MATERIALS NEEDED:
- [ ] Bible
- [ ] 3″ x 5″ file cards
- [ ] felt-tip pens (fine-tip)
- [ ] Scotch Tape
- [ ] notebook paper and pencils
- [ ] access to a basketball court (you could also adapt this easily for baseball, kickball, football, etc.)
- [ ] basketball (or whatever equipment you need)

TEXTS: Proverbs 12:20; 29:11

PREPARATION:
- [ ] Construct the table marker if desired. Write out Proverbs 12:20 on one side and 29:11 on the other.
- [ ] Think through several evidences of good sportsmanship. You will use these later to make a list. Also, depending on which sport you have chosen, think about specific ways you can use role playing to demonstrate good and bad sportsmanship in action.
- [ ] Decide how to divide your family into two teams for role playing.

FAMILY TIME:
1. During dinner, read the proverbs and discuss their wise advice. You might want to ask:

- **What does it mean to *promote* something?** (to actively urge and support)
- **What are some specific ways each of us can promote peace?** (seek compromise with family members and friends, ask forgiveness when wrong, not call anyone a name)
- **What does a fool do?** (lets his anger control *him*)
- **What does a wise man (or woman) do?** (he or she controls the *anger)*
- **Can you think of some times (when angry) you were not wise? When you were wise?**

2. Later, take several sheets of paper, pencils, and a ball to the court (or playground, field, parking lot, etc.).

3. Divide into two teams. Explain that each team will first be acting out a ball game played by team members who do not use good sportsmanship. Their role playing should include many examples. Next each team should repeat its skit, this time demonstrating correct attitudes and actions. Allow teams plenty of time to prepare.

4. Give each team two sheets of paper and a pencil. Ask them to print "Bad sports do these things" at the top of one sheet and "Good sports do these things" on the other. Then, while one team is role playing, the other team jots down attitudes and actions which fit under each category.

5. Take turns role playing and taking notes. Some of the specific attitudes and actions we noted for basketball were: making fun of another player, hogging the ball, calling names, bullying, allowing another to go first, helping another up off the floor, complimenting, being a gracious winner or loser.

6. When the teams have demonstrated both bad and good sportsmanship, sit in a circle and get out another sheet of paper. Label this sheet "Rules for Good Sports." Have team members suggest ideas from the lists which they have made. Some of the rules we listed were: be fair, pick fair teams, be kind, don't get revenge, don't hog the ball, remember teamwork and unselfishness, help others, don't be a sore loser or bad winner.

7. Then, relate your rules to the proverbs' advice of promoting peace and keeping anger under control. You might ask: **If another player shoves you, how do you *promote* peace? If you don't**

shove back, are you being foolish or wise? Use as many specific examples as you can.

8. Close in prayer, asking God to help us *do* these wise actions the next time we play a sport.

SUGGESTIONS:

Children between the ages of 7 and 11 often become so intensely competitive that playing a game with the family—any type of game—quickly turns from fun to frustrating. We watched this happen time after time until we *knew* we had to try something to improve behavior.

I can't say that this devotion will give immediate results—or guarantee *any* results, for that matter. Being intensely competitive is a stage of development children go through. This role playing, however, *does* give a graphic and visual reminder of how we should act when playing a game. And because our demonstration included *incorrect* and then *correct* behavior, it should give children hope that they can improve in their weak areas.

One of our sons committed Proverbs 29:11 to memory so that he could repeat it to himself whenever needed. I made a pact to memorize it with him, and then both of us would remind each other that "a fool...." Not surprisingly, there were several times when he *and Mom* did need that gentle reminder!

SERVICE: SECRET HELPERS

MATERIALS NEEDED:
- ☐ Bible
- ☐ 3″ x 5″ file cards
- ☐ felt-tip pens (fine-tip)
- ☐ Scotch Tape

TEXT: Philippians 2:3-8

PREPARATION:

☐ Construct the table marker, writing out Philippians 2:3-8. You may also want to make one with "Secret Helpers?" written on each side.

☐ Read and study Philippians 2:3-8.

☐ Think about several suggestions of ways your children can secretly serve another family member. For example, one could secretly make another's bed or pick up the room, feed the dog, sweep a porch, etc. Be sure to have several possibilities that can be done quickly enough so that no one else would find out who had performed that task.

FAMILY TIME:

1. At dinner, take turns reading Philippians 2:3-8 verse by verse.

2. Lead a discussion about these verses. You may want to ask questions like:

- **What are *incorrect* motives (reasons) for serving others?** (to build up myself and my reputation, to make myself look good)
- **What are *correct* motives?** (with humility, loving others so much that I put their needs before mine)
- **Whose example are we to follow?** (that of Christ—who became a servant)

3. Later, begin with prayer.

4. Announce that you are all going to be Secret Helpers for one day. Build interest by emphasizing that everything you do must be done with *absolute* secrecy: no one in the family can see when someone else has been helped. Ask that each family member do at

least one kind and helpful task for someone else in the family; you can do more if you wish. If someone gets "caught," he or she will need to do something else.

5. Refer to the verses in Philippians and review by asking how and why we should serve one another. Again, be sure to emphasize that we put others before ourselves because of our love for them and because of Christ's example of love for us.

6. Make sure that everyone has some ideas that he or she can do. If not, give the suggestions which you thought of earlier.

7. Close in prayer, asking God to help us be true servants.

8. *During dinner the next evening:* First, make sure that everyone has been a Secret Helper. *Do not* allow anyone to share what he or she did; announce that our activities must remain a secret forever!

9. Then, concentrate on the feelings we have when we serve someone else. You might say: **Pretend that you are doing that task right now. How do you feel?** (warm, happy, fulfilled, excited) **Now you know that no one will ever know that you did that task. No one will ever thank you for doing it. Now how do you feel?** (maybe frustrated, disappointed, but still happy)

10. Discuss how this can be a measure of our reasons for serving, or our motivations. If we served only to receive a "thank you," then we did not put others before ourselves.

11. You might want to pray again concerning servanthood, asking God to help us know if our motivations are to serve others—or ourselves.

SUGGESTIONS:

Living as a family, day in and day out, certainly must be the greatest test of Christian maturity. I guess we just get so used to being with each other and take each other so much for granted that we allow relationship-building (and I mean true edification) to slide. I constantly must remind myself—doesn't my family deserve just as much active, positive effort as I give to other relationships? And even *more?*

This family time gave us the motivation and reason we needed to actively *be nice to each other!* Once enforced, we found that it was not so terribly difficult, and as a matter of fact we also learned insights about ourselves. (How many times have I caught myself lately, thinking, "He didn't even notice . . . !")

It's interesting too how each time our family does something like this (Servant Jar and Secret Pals are similar in concept), everyone gets more creative and enthusiastic. In the future—do I dare think it?—could we all actually do nice things for each other without even being asked?

REVENGE: GODLY PATIENCE

MATERIALS NEEDED:

- [ ] Bible
- [ ] 3″ x 5″ file cards
- [ ] felt-tip pens (fine-tip)
- [ ] Scotch Tape
- [ ] stapler and staples
- [ ] pencils
- [ ] the song "Patience" from *The Music Machine* (by Candle, Sparrow Records, Inc., 1977)

TEXT: Galatians 5:22-23

PREPARATION:

- [ ] Construct the table marker, writing out Galatians 5:22-23. Underline for emphasis the word *patience* or use another color of felt-tip pen to make the word *patience* stand out.

- [ ] Listen to "Patience" from *The Music Machine.* Set it aside for use later along with file cards (enough for each member of the family to have one), pencils, stapler, and staples.

- [ ] Think through suggestions for your children of times when someone may commit a wrong toward them, but when they should not seek revenge. Some examples may be teasing from a sibling, being pushed or shoved during a ball game, or being called a name.

FAMILY TIME:

1. During dinner, read Galatians 5:22-23. If you have memorized this in the past, take turns reciting the verses. Or you may want to commit it to memory at this time. Point out that you will be discussing *patience* and what this word really means.

2. Later, have everyone sit near the tape/record/CD player and begin with prayer.

3. You may want to begin by asking: **What do *you* think the word *patience* means?** (Not getting grumpy, allowing others to go first, and waiting calmly in line may be some of the answers that you get.)

4. Play "Patience" to see what Herbert the snail says patience is. (You may want to play the song a couple of times.)

5. Explain that the word *patience* in Galatians 5:22 means much more than merely being considerate while waiting for someone else. Actually, *godly patience* means not seeking revenge when someone has committed a wrong against you. So, if someone hits you, you don't seek revenge and strike back. Then you might ask: **What specific examples of godly patience can you think of?** (Give some examples to help them think, if necessary. Or lead them to suggestions by asking: **What about on the playground? On the bus?**)

6. Hand out a 3″ x 5″ card and pencil to each family member. Ask everyone to write: "I will try to have godly patience when . . ." and then continue to fill in the response. Emphasize that we need to be specific about what we want to do.

7. Fold and staple the cards closed.

8. Put the cards into a pile and have each person pick one. (If anyone accidentally gets his or her own card, just exchange it.) Open the cards; take turns praying for that person and his or her desire to demonstrate godly patience.

SUGGESTIONS:

The idea for this devotion came about when Craig was preparing to teach the fruits of the Spirit to a Vacation Bible School class. Researching the meaning and background of the words, he was excited to find their meanings more explicit than what we had assumed them to be. I remember his telling me that some would be difficult to teach, but "*Patience,*" he said, "will be one they'll really relate to."

When we used the idea for a family devotion, we found that we all related well too, listing many examples of times when we should demonstrate godly patience. The emphasis can shift from family to friendships outside the home to how we relate and act toward whomever we meet throughout the day. (I can vividly remember deciding to use godly patience while driving the car and when maneuvering the shopping cart through the aisles at the store!)

This is another example of when parents must set an example of honesty and vulnerability. Because Craig and I shared specific responses which were true convictions, the boys could follow our lead. As parents, this is one of the steps of the tremendous responsibility and privilege that we have—to guide our children along the pathway to truly open, honest, and vulnerable relationships before their Lord.

SUFFERING: MAGIC NIGHT—JESUS REVEALED!

MATERIALS NEEDED:

- [ ] Bible
- [ ] 3″ x 5″ file cards
- [ ] felt-tip pens (fine-tip)
- [ ] books which teach simple magic tricks, such as sleight-of-hand disappearing tricks (I found several appropriate books at the local library.)
- [ ] a top hat and baton, if available
- [ ] any supplies which you will need for the magic tricks

TEXT: 1 Peter 4:12-13

PREPARATION:

- [ ] Construct the table marker, writing out 1 Peter 4:12-13.
- [ ] Study 1 Peter 4:12-13 by cross-referencing (see Rom. 8:18-19, 1 John 3:1-2, and 1 Peter 5:1). Concentrate on the word *revealed,* which means the future manifestation of the glory that is *already present in us.*
- [ ] Bring home several magic tricks books from the library.
- [ ] At least one or two days before your family night, tell everyone to choose a trick from the available books. Each family member is to practice and perform one trick of his or her choice. Tricks that reveal something that was already hidden, however, are preferred. (Tell them to *practice* their tricks.)
- [ ] Choose a magic trick for yourself also. It should definitely be one that appears to make something disappear but instead, reveals that the object was there all the time—just hidden from sight. I suggest you choose a trick that is relatively simple.
- [ ] Collect any needed materials for your magic trick and practice it several times.

FAMILY TIME:

1. At dinner read the verses and lead a discussion about any suffering (related to suffering for being a Christian) that members of the family may be experiencing. For example, schoolchildren may be teasing your kids because they do not use swear words or get

into fights on the playground. Dad may not be getting a much-deserved bigger office because he wouldn't bad-mouth a fellow worker to receive it. The whole family may be doing without a new car in order to continue giving at church.

2. Relate how these times are to be expected (v. 12), and even to be rejoiced in (v. 13), because in this way we identify with Christ. Emphasize that these *prove* our Christianity and bring us closer to Him.

3. Then, build interest and curiosity by alluding to your Magic Night with a statement something like this: **As we'll witness with our very own eyes tonight at the greatest magic show on earth, what will be *revealed* is *glorious!***

4. Later, gather everyone for your Magic Night. Have everyone bring his or her needed supplies for the magic tricks. You may want to arrange chairs so that you have a "stage" and audience area. Some sort of table will probably be necessary.

5. As Master of Ceremonies (with top hat and baton if available), begin with something like this: **Ladies and gentlemen! We are here to witness one of the greatest magic shows ever seen. Our first act is the truly amazing** *(give the title of the act)* **by** *(give the child's name).* **And now, to present this wondrous feat . . . I give you . . .** *(name)!*

6. Be sure to give rounds of applause as each child completes his act—whether successfully or not.

7. Lastly, perform your trick of "revealing" what only appears to be placed elsewhere. Repeat it several times and then teach everyone how the trick works. (Your children may want to try doing the trick also.)

8. Put the magic trick materials aside and gather in a circle on the floor.

9. Emphasize strongly that, just like the object that could not be seen but was *there all the time,* Jesus also is *always* with us. Reread 1 Peter 4:12-13 and teach them the meaning of the word *revealed.* Try to capture the wonder and promise in those words that, no matter what sufferings we may have to endure now, He is with us, and will one glorious day be revealed for all to see.

10. Pray for each other—asking for strength during tough times and wisdom to *know* He is there.

SUGGESTIONS:

A dear friend of mine was studying the word *revealed* when she became so excited about the meaning that came alive to her. Wanting to pass on this feeling to her children, she came up with the idea of a magic trick that would graphically teach the idea that even though we can't *see* something, that does not mean it does not exist. And what better pattern could there be for a family devotion—a personal devotion so exciting that we want to share it with our loved ones?

When our family did this, Craig used one of those pictures that, because of black and white shading, you must concentrate to see that two pictures exist in one. I used a simple trick with a coin in a box that also applied the principle of "revealed." Both helped the boys grasp the principle of Jesus' presence with us, and especially during those lonely times of suffering.

We also wanted our sons to see suffering as a positive experience rather than a negative one. By emphasizing to them that their suffering proves that they are Christians (and we were proud of them for "sticking out" this way in a crowd), I think they did see suffering with new eyes. And those "new eyes" also included the ability to see another Person right beside them—One who will be revealed someday!

RESPONSIBILITY: GROWN-UP NIGHT

MATERIALS NEEDED:
- [ ] 3″ x 5″ file cards
- [ ] felt-tip pens (fine-tip)
- [ ] Scotch Tape
- [ ] sewing supplies: needles, thread, buttons, material, scissors
- [ ] groceries for a supper that your children can make (for example: eggs, muffin mix, potatoes, bacon, plus the necessary pots and pans, etc.)
- [ ] access to a washer and dryer, detergent, and dirty clothes
- [ ] dishes that your children will wash (unbreakable, if available)

PREPARATION:

[ ] Construct the table marker, writing out *Grown-up Night* on each side.

[ ] Prepare sewing supplies so that each member of the family can sew on a button and sew a hem.

[ ] Make sure that there is a wide assortment of dirty clothes to be sorted and washed.

[ ] Plan an evening meal that will be a challenge, but not too difficult, for your children to prepare. Make sure that you have on hand all the necessary ingredients and pots and pans.

FAMILY TIME:

1. About an hour before normal dinner time, announce that your children will be "chief cooks" tonight. Put it in very upbeat and positive terms; convey the idea of what an exciting privilege—and fun adventure—this will be.

2. Carefully explain exactly what they will be responsible for making and also that you will be available to help at any point. You may especially need to help get them started, but then watch them take off on their own!

3. Ask them to set the table also. Be sure to place the table marker in the center.

4. Later, while enjoying your *delicious* meal (and you *must* em-

phasize what a yummy meal they have prepared), describe what else Grown-up Night will entail: learning to sew a button and hem, to sort and wash clothes, and wash dishes.

5. After the dishes have been washed (with a little parental help), take family members to the laundry room and teach them to sort darks, whites, and colors for washing. Explain the settings on the washer and dryer: temperature, water level, fabric type, and how to set the timer. At this point you may or may not want to actually wash a load or two of clothes.

6. Next, gather around the table to begin learning to sew on a button and how to sew a hem. You may even have some clothes that need a button sewn on. Be sure to include how to match the color of the thread to the material, how to thread the needle, tie a knot, and where to begin sewing on the button and the hem.

7. End your evening with praise for your children for how independent and grown-up they are to be able to make supper, clean up, wash clothes, and sew.

8. Close with prayer, thanking God that one day your children will be grown-up and responsible adults.

SUGGESTIONS:

I felt convicted to do this devotional when I realized how lax I had been recently about teaching our sons to prepare for the future. Too often I find it easier just to do things myself rather than take the time to teach them important skills. And it is *never* easy for me to volunteer my kitchen for a two-man demolition team! So I thought through several tasks that I realized were necessary and attempted to make doing them fun.

These tasks *did* turn out to be much fun. The boys thoroughly enjoyed being the chief cooks. We even heard them humming merrily—until they had to flip the eggs, that is. The boys were even interested in all the buttons on the washer and dryer; they were *not* interested in Dad's dirty socks—whew! Later we all stitched away at buttons and hems after several tries at tying a knot.

It was a very successful evening for us and one that put my mind at ease somewhat too. I hope now when they go off to college, they won't be among those freshmen who dump bleach into a load of dark socks and jeans.

ARGUING: SKIT NIGHT

MATERIALS NEEDED:
- ☐ Bible
- ☐ 3″ x 5″ file cards
- ☐ felt-tip pens (fine-tip)
- ☐ Scotch Tape
- ☐ props for skits, if desired

TEXT: Proverbs 15:1

PREPARATION:

☐ Construct the table marker, writing out Proverbs 15:1.

☐ Think through the meaning of verse 1 and ways that you can relate this to your children. For example, when another child calls your child a name, he or she should not react by also calling a name. Instead your child might respond by ignoring the name-calling, or by merely saying, "That's not nice."

☐ Parents, you must plan and rehearse ahead of time the skits which you will be performing. We planned two "negative" skits: one in which *I* was grumpy when Craig came home in a good mood, and one in which *Craig* came home grumpy and *I* was in a good mood. Both were designed to show how a bad mood can be "catching" if family members are not careful. We then planned two "positive" skits which showed how we *should* have responded to each other's moods.

One of our "negative" skits went something like this:

Mom is banging cupboards and pans very loudly as she makes supper.
Dad comes in the front door from work, whistling happily: Hi! I'm home!
(No response except more banging)
Dad to Mom: So, how was your day?
Mom, curtly: Fine.
Dad, sensing trouble: Oh. So what's for dinner?
Mom, curtly: Food.
Dad, peeking into a pot, and reaching for a spoon for a taste:

Hey, this smells good.
Mom, with agitation: Stay out of that! It's not ready yet!
Dad, meekly: I just wanted a little taste.
Mom: Now you're in my way!
Dad, now beginning to get a bit testy himself: I just thought I'd help a little if you were tired!
Mom: Who said I was tired? I feel just fine! Just fine!
Dad: Well, you certainly don't . . . (fading).
Mom, excitedly: What was that? What are you saying?
Dad: Nothing! Nothing at all!
Mom: Well, you certainly don't need to come home and take out your bad day on me!
Dad, defensively: Bad day? I came home in a good mood! It's *your* fault if I'm grumpy now!
Mom: *My* fault? I was in a fine mood until you started poking around in the kitchen! Now look at us!

Then, our "positive" skit went something like this:

Again, Mom is banging pots and pans in the kitchen.
Dad comes in the front door from work, whistling merrily: Hi! I'm home! What's for supper?
Mom, curtly: Food!
Dad, responding to her obvious weariness: Sounds like you could use a little extra help in here. What can I do? Set the table?
Mom, sighing with relief: That would be great. . . .

Be sure to plan skits that fit *your personalities* and will drive home the point that "a gentle answer turns away wrath."

FAMILY TIME:
1. During dinner, read Proverbs 15:1 and discuss ways each member of the family can implement this at work, school, play, church, etc.
2. Later, announce to your children that the "world's best actor and actress" will be presenting several plays. You may want to title each one of your skits.
3. Be sure to follow the negative example with a strong *positive*

example skit. This way the correct responses are the last ones your children see, leaving a more lasting impression.

4. Have a time of discussion when you emphasize how "grumpiness" can spread like an infectious disease—unless *someone* takes the initiative to give *gentle answers.* Point out what the specific "gentle answers" were and how they helped to bring peace to what obviously could become an argumentative situation.

5. Close in prayer, asking God to help everyone in the family respond kindly to one another, instead of with wrath.

SUGGESTIONS:

Have you ever noticed, as we did, how grumpiness does indeed spread like a disease from one family member to another? If not checked, soon the whole family can come down with a severe case of the grumps.

If our children had been cranky on the evening that Craig and I did this, they would surely have cheered up quickly, for they were nearly rolling on the floor with laughter at Mom and Dad's banter! But believe me, they got the point well enough too; the "catchability" of the grumpiness was too graphic to be missed. (NOTE: Single parents, you can easily adapt this for use by having one of your children play one of the parent roles.) Our kids also related well themselves, understanding that they both "spread" the grumps on occasion too.

I especially like the concept of this family time because it reinforces that we are not at the mercy of our feelings; we can make a *choice* to do something about cranky feelings. Choosing to respond to another with gentle words is an active decision that I can make and one that I definitely want to pass on to our sons. It can make all the difference by resulting in a miserable home—or a *joyful* one.

PREJUDICE: CHOCOLATE COOKIES AND OTHER DILEMMAS

MATERIALS NEEDED:
- ☐ Bible
- ☐ 3″ x 5″ file cards
- ☐ felt-tip pens (broad- and- fine tip)
- ☐ Scotch Tape
- ☐ construction paper
- ☐ ingredients for chocolate cookies:
  2 c. white sugar
  ½ c. cocoa
  ½ c. milk
  ½ c. butter or margarine
  1 tsp. vanilla
  3 c. quick oats
  1 c. chopped nuts, if desired
  (Instructions: Boil sugar, cocoa, milk, butter, and vanilla together for five minutes. Mix well with quick oats and nuts. Quickly drop by spoonfuls onto waxed paper and cool.)

TEXT: Acts 10:34-35

PREPARATION:
- ☐ Construct the table marker, writing out Acts 10:34-35.
- ☐ Gather ingredients, measuring spoons, pans, and mixing spoons so that all will be readily available later.
- ☐ Think through any prejudices you may have or your children may have so that you can discuss these (and how irrational and unfounded they are) during Family Time. Try to recall less obvious ones also, such as: "all handicapped people have intellectual defects" and "those who talk slowly are mentally slow also."
- ☐ On a piece of construction paper, write out: "Prejudice—an opinion made before the facts are known."

FAMILY TIME:
1. During dinner read Acts 10:34-35, and ask questions like:
- **Does God show favoritism?**

- **Whom does God accept?**
- **If God accepts men and women from every nation, what are some of the races of people of the world that He accepts?**
- **Does He love one race more than another? Why or why not, do you think?**

Try to have a frank and honest discussion about God's unconditional love and justice and why these characteristics lead Him to love all people equally.

2. After dinner, announce something like this: **We're going to make some cookies that by all appearances look absolutely horrible! Whether you taste them or not will be *your* decision. *You* must decide whether to risk your health by eating these grotesque, strange-looking chocolate cookies!**

3. Allow the entire family to measure, mix, and cook the cookies. After dropping them onto the waxed paper, slip them into the refrigerator for quick cooling.

4. Set a cookie in front of each member of the family. Again tease them about the "horrible looks" of the cookies, but go ahead and enjoy eating one yourself! Hopefully, your children will hesitate to taste them, but then eventually muster the courage to take a bite. When they discover how delicious they really are, enjoy several and the fellowship time together.

5. Take out your sheet of paper with the definition of prejudice on it. Have one child read it and then relate this definition to the experience with the cookies. Explain how prejudices about all sorts of things occur in the exact same way—with our making decisions about things before all facts are known. Have your children list as many prejudices as they can think of—ones others have and ones *they* may have.

6. Drive home the point again that these prejudices are just as unfounded as the idea that the cookies you just made must be awful.

7. Remind them also that *God especially* shows no favoritism or prejudice toward mankind—and thus neither should we.

8. Close in prayer, asking for wisdom to know what prejudices we may still have and need to dispel. Ask for unconditional love for everyone.

SUGGESTIONS:

Many years ago, when our sons were still toddlers, I made a batch of these cookies. When we discovered that we had to literally *force* them to try them (being typical kids, of course, they wouldn't try anything that looked so different), it occurred to me that *this* was a perfect example of prejudice. No amount of rationalizing or pleading could entice the boys to try those cookies; they had made up their minds on incorrect data and would not budge. Isn't that a perfect picture of prejudice—prior judgment made on false data—with no possibility of anyone convincing me otherwise, either. (Don't confuse me with the facts; I've made up my mind!)

Our challenge, then, is to first realize that we do indeed have prejudices and to surface and dispel them. Only through honest dialogue with ourselves (through conviction) and others such as family members (who can be invaluable resources in this area), can we begin to tackle this problem in our lives.

By the way, our sons have now decided that they do like those cookies. But I'm afraid the nickname for them has become another opportunity to tease Mom. (Why do I set myself up for these things?) The first question I hear when the boys come home from school is, "Hey, Mom! Do we have any more of those *absolutely awful* cookies?"

EMOTIONS: HOW DO I FEEL WHEN . . . ?

MATERIALS NEEDED:
- ☐ several blank sheets of paper
- ☐ crayons or felt-tip pens (fine-tip)
- ☐ one, two, or three pertinent questions

PREPARATION:

☐ Decide on some pertinent questions for your family members to help them describe their feelings with a picture. Some of the questions which we have addressed are:
- What is my strongest feeling this week?
- How do I feel when someone in the family is grumpy?
- How do I (parents/kids) feel when the kids have homework?
- How do I feel when I'm home alone?
- How do I feel when I'm pressured or stressed?
- How do I feel when I lose a game?
- How do I feel when (parents/kids) argue?
- How do I feel when Mom has to nag me to do something?
- What was my (happiest/lowest) feeling this week?

Try to choose questions that are pertinent to the needs of your family by being sensitive to each individual's moods. When we noticed that our children were responding negatively to our "helter-skelter" rush-about week, we decided to find out what feelings they were experiencing. When playing a game became a miserable experience because one son could not tolerate losing, we asked the question on losing a game. Sometimes we just want a lighter sharing, and then we'll write and draw a picture of the happiest feeling experienced this week. *Whatever* we share, the rewards of knowing each other's feelings better are always present.

FAMILY TIME:

1. Have everyone sit around the table.
2. Hand out several sheets of paper to each person.
3. Put many different colors of crayons or fine-tip markers in the center of the table.
4. Announce that family members will be writing a brief description and then drawing pictures about their feelings on a particular

question. Explain that participants need to concentrate on digging out feelings which are "underneath their feelings." This means that rarely do we feel merely sad, mad, happy, or scared. For *underneath* these basic feelings are deeper ones—possibly loneliness, frustration, lightheartedness, or depression. These *deeper* feelings are a true indication of what is really going on inside us.

5. Explain that the picture we draw should be a depiction of a situation that shows how we feel. For example, if I say I feel sad, and underneath my sadness I feel lonely, my picture might be a drawing of myself in a huge crowd of people—but I know no one and no one is paying any attention to me. If I feel mad, and underneath this I feel pressured, I might draw myself in the middle of a vice that is closing tighter and tighter.

6. Ask the feeling question and allow everyone plenty of time to complete his or her picture.

7. When everyone has finished, share your pictures by describing the feelings and the drawings. Repeat for other questions.

8. Close in prayer.

SUGGESTIONS:

For seven wonderful years, Craig and I were a presenting pastoral couple for Baptist Expression of Marriage Encounter. This tremendous organization changed our lives by teaching us skills we had not possessed before: the ability to dig out feelings and share them with each other and our children. The practice of sharing our feelings with our children—and our children sharing with us—has proved to be an invaluable tool.

Too often we merely assume that feelings will be shared, even if we are conscious of their existence and do try to be open. However, only when we actually *set aside a specific time* to share our feelings does this come about in our home. Otherwise, these important feelings get lost in the hustle-bustle of the everyday.

The feelings reveal the *person* behind them—what he or she is experiencing deep down inside. That is invaluable information to a parent of a hurting child, an angry child, or a lonely child. Our sharing times have given us insight, joy, revelation, and sympathetic understanding. I pray this will become as valuable a tool for you as it has become for us.

Eight
SERVICE/CONCERN

SERVANT JAR

MATERIALS NEEDED:
- ☐ Bible
- ☐ jar (with lid)
- ☐ construction paper
- ☐ felt-tip pens
- ☐ 3″ x 5″ cards
- ☐ pencils
- ☐ tape

TEXTS: Genesis 45—Joseph's story. Also, review chapters 37 through 45 so that you can relate to your children the wondrous story of Joseph's childhood—his coat, dreams, selling by his brothers, imprisonment, eventual appointment by Pharaoh, and reuniting with his brothers and father.

John 13:1-17—Jesus washing the disciples' feet

PREPARATION:

☐ Decorate jar with construction paper. Label it "Servant Jar."

☐ For each member of the family, write each of these statements on a separate 3″ x 5″ card:

1. "I will be a servant tonight by _____."

2. "I will be a servant this week by _____."

☐ Construct table marker. If you choose the story of Joseph, you may want to write out Genesis 37:9. This verse could then be used to introduce the subject of Joseph, his dreams, and the out-come. If you choose John 13, write out verse 5 and do some background study of foot-washing during biblical times. (Resources for additional help are listed at the back of this book.)

☐ Choose one passage and study it.

FAMILY TIME:

1. Open with prayer.

2. Read the Bible passage and discuss the examples of servanthood demonstrated by Jesus or Joseph. If you are discussing Jesus, attempt to help your children understand the supreme example of humility modeled here. Relate what a lowly and humbling duty this was, and even more so for the Son of God. Ask: **Why do you think Jesus did this?** (as an example to us) **How do you feel thinking about Jesus doing this for you? Does it make you want to do anything?** (serve Him and others)

3. For Joseph's story, capture their attention with the reuniting of Joseph and his brothers. Ask: **Will Joseph seek revenge? Will he make them suffer now for what they did to him? Doesn't he have the *right* to do this?** Finally, drive home the amazing conclusion that not only does Joseph not seek retribution, but he demonstrates a servant's spirit toward his brothers' needs by eventually providing a place to live and food to eat.

4. Ask: **How and where does God want us to be servants?** Be sure to cover specifics of *attitudes* (not serving with a grudge, doing things merely out of duty, searching for quick ways to finish the "chore") and *places we can serve* (school—helping friends with schoolwork; play—sharing favorite toys; church—helping teacher pick up the crayons; community—putting trash in a trash can rather than on the ground; home—helping Mom set the table for dinner).

5. Draw out as many specific ideas and attitudes toward serving as possible. For example, also ask: **How do we feel when we serve others?** (happy, fulfilled, joyful) **When others *notice* our efforts?** (proud, secure) **When they *don't* notice?** (resentful, unappreciated) **How do we feel when others serve us?** (possibly embarrassed or even uncomfortable)

6. Introduce the "Servant Jar" as a wonderful opportunity. **Now we can be God's servants!** Discuss the important commitment of

deciding to serve in a specific way tonight. Help your children by listing several examples of how each one can serve another member of the family—doing dishes, helping with homework, etc. Be sure to have them sign their names as a pledge.

7. Ask each person to choose one means of service to perform for another, and to write his or her pledge on a 3″ x 5″ card, being sure to sign it. Each one should put the folded card into the jar and remember to keep this a secret. Discuss committing to serve this week. Next, have family members fill out other cards, writing their promises to serve. These should also be kept secret, folded, and put into the jar. (You may want to mark these in some way to identify them as next week's cards.)

8. Ask for prayer requests and pray that family members will learn to develop servanthood.

9. Later remove cards for tonight's commitment.

10. Discuss what you did and how this felt to everyone.

11. Remind everyone of commitments for the coming week. Discussion for these will be at the beginning of next week's devotions.

SUGGESTIONS:

This was a devotional that initially came about because of a noticeable "me first" attitude around our home. Not too surprisingly, we have repeated this exercise a few times since then. It has worked well because we all benefit in parallel ways: we learn by serving and we are blessed by receiving.

I think the practice of signing our names to the commitments has been helpful too. Somehow that lends an air of importance and seriousness to what we're doing. The kids don't take this one lightly; they fulfill their "contracts" happily.

We also had good discussions concerning serving—when the other person noticed the service and when he or she did not, when our acts were appreciated and when they were not—and how this does or does not change our acts of continued service. For example, we asked questions like, "Should we *expect* a thank-you? Do we serve only those who appreciate us? Should we stop serving someone who does not?" We also discussed our feelings in all of these situations. Of course, the ultimate standard of servanthood is Jesus Christ, so we compared His servanthood with our efforts.

I must add a quick note of warning to this one. Sometimes what a child considers helping can be something quite different to Mom and Dad. Case in point: our younger pledged to help by assisting us in painting his room. Mom and Dad had to exercise great amounts of patience as he "helped" that evening!

WORLD RELIEF NIGHT

MATERIALS NEEDED:
- [ ] Bible
- [ ] 3″ x 5″ file cards
- [ ] felt-tip pens (fine-tip)
- [ ] Scotch Tape
- [ ] chopsticks
- [ ] an envelope, plus an offering of the money you will save by eating just rice for supper (to be given to your church or a relief organization)
- [ ] a plain meal of rice (with some vegetables in it), milk, bread (no butter)
- [ ] encyclopedias or magazines with pictures of Third World children or other children who are victims of malnutrition

TEXT: Galatians 2:10

PREPARATION:
- [ ] Construct the table marker, writing out Galatians 2:10.
- [ ] Find several pictures of children which dramatically portray the plight of the poor in this world. Set these aside for later.
- [ ] Make your simple meal of rice. (I put in some celery and onions to add nutrition since this was to be our only meal for the evening.)
- [ ] On a plain envelope write out, "World Relief Offering."
- [ ] Set the table with bowls, cups, chopsticks, and plain bread.

FAMILY TIME:

1. At dinner announce that tonight family members will be eating what many of the children of the world have for each and every meal—if they are fortunate enough to have *this much.* Serve the rice and enjoy eating with chopsticks!

2. Read Galatians 2:10 and discuss how Paul was eager to care for the poor. You might want to ask questions like: **How can we as a family care for the poor? What about tonight? What can we**

do with the money we're saving by not having a regular evening meal?

3. Show the pictures of the starving children that you have collected. These should generate many questions and, therefore, a good discussion about world hunger and concern for the needy should follow.

4. Bring out the "World Relief Offering" envelope. Tell the children that you as parent(s) will be putting in an offering for tonight. Ask them if they also would like to contribute. Be sure to tell them *where* the money will be going—to the world relief fund of your choice.

5. Close in prayer by praying for the poor of our world and asking that we be sensitive and responsive to their needs.

SUGGESTIONS:

This devotion was an odd combination in that we had fun and difficulty using chopsticks for the first time (though where there's a will, there's a way), yet the graphic pictures of starving children were very sobering to all of us. The responsibility to help the poor can be overwhelming, but we did feel like we were at least making a *beginning* by doing without in order to give.

The boys did not complain about the sparse meal (except for a surprised "Where's the butter?"). As a matter of fact, they seemed to take this as a matter of *duty*. This was something that they wanted to do to help. We were glad that we could have a time of fellowship together and experience the joy of giving.

Nine
JUST FUN

SCAVENGER HUNT

MATERIALS NEEDED:
- ☐ notebook paper
- ☐ pens/pencils/crayons or felt-tip pens
- ☐ construction paper (white)
- ☐ popcorn and soft drinks

PREPARATION:

☐ Write out two copies of the Scavenger Hunt list. Ours listed these things:

1. a dead bug
2. a paper clip
3. a yellow crayon
4. have Bo (our dog) shake hands; give him a cookie
5. a bow (the kind for a wrapped present)
6. both sing "The Star-Spangled Banner"
7. a piece of lint (*not* from the laundry room)
8. Draw a picture of a leprechaun. (We did this in March). The best picture gets credit.
9. a dirty sock (*not* one you're wearing!)
10. a toothpick
11. throw Bo's ball for him; give him another cookie
12. a map
13. both blow a bubble (find gum first)
14. a square of toilet paper
15. go outside; yell, "This family is crazy!"

16. kiss Mom
17. punch Dad
18. shake hands with Robb
19. give Jay "five"
20. hug Bo

☐ Make one copy of rules. Please have fun creating your own rules to fit your unique family. Let your imagination go! Our rules list went like this:

1. No bad sports (no *grumping!*) allowed.
2. No pushing, shoving, running, or stealing of other team's items allowed.
3. Teams must *stay together,* and you can't go one at a time to get things.
4. You don't need to go in order of the list.
5. Losers must serve winners popcorn and pop—fix plus clean up; losers get to eat too!
6. Sore losers must run around the house 10 times.
7. Since Mom made up the game, she makes judgment calls ("seems fair to me").
8. *Everyone* helps put items away at end of game. (Bo must put away his toys!)

☐ Check to see that whatever you put on the list is available. Supply two boxes (for teams' collected items), construction paper, and crayons for pictures, if needed.

FAMILY TIME:

1. Open with prayer.
2. Read and explain the rules; answer any questions. Divide into teams.
3. Give teams the lists and boxes.
4. *Ready, set . . . have fun!*
5. Share about the hilarious moments while munching popcorn.
6. Close in prayer, thanking God for family and fun.

SUGGESTIONS:

Whenever I reminisce about fun family times, this Scavenger Hunt inevitably comes to mind. I enjoyed putting it together, but then the actual participation was even more fun! We nearly laughed ourselves silly at each other, and especially our crazy dog! No, this family time did not really accomplish anything . . . or did it? For we fellowshipped in the joy of our love and friendship for each other, and we thoroughly enjoyed being together as a family. And that *is* accomplishing much!

CLUE QUEST

MATERIALS NEEDED:
- [ ] Bible
- [ ] 3″ x 5″ file cards
- [ ] pen or fine-tip marker
- [ ] masking tape
- [ ] popcorn and drinks or special dessert

PREPARATION:

[ ] Prepare your Clue Quest by using your Bible's concordance. To do this, think of places outside (or inside) where you can send your family on its quest. For example, if you have a birdbath or feeder, you may want to look up a reference for a Bible verse containing the word *bird.* When you have found a verse in the concordance that contains the word *bird,* write out the verse on a 3″ x 5″ card. This card, then, will be the clue card to send your family to the birdbath, where they will find the card for their *next* clue.

[ ] Here are the clues and solutions we used for our Clue Quest:

1. "For whoever is joined with the living, there is hope; surely a live dog is better than a dead lion" Ecclesiastes 9:4. (They were to guess the *dog's house,* where I had taped the card with the next clue.)
2. "How beautiful are the feet of those who bring glad tidings of good things!" Romans 10:15b (the mailbox)
3. "Look at the birds of the air, that they do not sow, neither do they reap, nor gather into barns, and yet your Heavenly Father feeds them. Are you not worth much more than they?" Matthew 6:26 (bird feeder)
4. "And so when they got out upon the land, they saw a charcoal fire already laid, and fish placed upon it, and bread" John 21:9. (charcoal grill)
5. "And you pay special attention to the one who is wearing the fine clothes, and say, 'You sit here in a good place,' and you say to the poor man, 'You stand over there, or sit down by my footstool'" James 2:3. (clothesline)

6. "And it came about in due time, after Hannah had conceived, that she gave birth to a son; and she named him Samuel, saying, 'Because I have asked him of the Lord'" 1 Samuel 1:20. (our car—which is named Samuel)

7. "But you, when you pray, go into your inner room, and when you have shut your door, pray to your Father who is in secret, and your Father who sees in secret will repay you" Matthew 6:6. (the front door)

8. "Then she let them down by a rope through the window, for her house was on the city wall, so that she was living on the wall" Joshua 2:15. (a window)

9. "Now the slaves and the officers were standing there, having made a charcoal fire, for it was cold and they were warming themselves; and Peter also was with them, standing and warming himself" John 18:18. (woodpile)

10. "Jesus spoke to them, saying, 'I am the Light of the world; he who follows Me shall not walk in darkness, but shall have the light of life'" John 8:12. (door light)

11. "But the disciples were indignant when they saw this and said, 'What is the point of this waste?'" Matthew 26:8 (This one's my favorite—the trash can!)

12. "For we shall surely die and are like water spilled on the ground" 2 Samuel 14:14a. (water faucet)

13. "Take your ease, eat, drink, and be merry!" Luke 12:19b (dessert time!)

☐ Once you have written out all of your cards, you will need to place them at the correct stations. *Be careful.* Remember that the clue for the bird feeder, for example, is *not put on the bird feeder!* The *next* clue, the clue for the charcoal grill, is taped onto the bird feeder! Do them in order to avoid confusion.

☐ Last, prepare that special dessert for your fellowship time together.

FAMILY TIME:

1. Announce that it is time for a Clue Quest. Explain that each card contains a Bible verse with a clue to where family members should look for the next clue. You might want to advise them to *guess* before racing off to where they judge the next station to be.

This could save them a good deal of fruitless searching.

2. When your family has completed the entire quest, enjoy a time of fellowshipping together while munching on dessert.

SUGGESTIONS:

The pandemonium as kids, dog, and parents raced around the house, down the hill to the mailbox, back up again to tear here and there was quite a riot! Our neighbors may have thought we had lost our senses once again, but who cares? We had a ball!

Be sure to use your imagination for this one; it's very easy to use your concordance in many creative ways. Just tailor your Clue Quest for your home and watch your family enjoy it tremendously.

SHOE GAME

MATERIALS NEEDED:
- ☐ Bible
- ☐ 3″ x 5″ file cards
- ☐ felt-tip pens (fine-tip)
- ☐ Scotch Tape
- ☐ at least three pairs of shoes from each member of the family
- ☐ a Bible for each member of the family

PREPARATION:

☐ Construct the table marker, writing out only the references for these verses:

1. Romans 10:15
2 Exodus 12:11
3. Acts 7:33
4. Psalm 119:105
5. Mark 1:7
6. Deuteronomy 29:5
7. Matthew 3:11
8. Psalm 40:2
9. Amos 2:6
10. Matthew 10:10

FAMILY TIME:

1. It must be dark to play the Shoe Game, so when it is dark outside, ask everyone to get his or her Bible.

2. Announce that later we will be playing a fun game in the dark, but family members must first guess what game we'll be playing. The clues to this secret game can be found in all of the verses on the table marker. Read off the references one at a time, allowing everyone to look up and then read the verse. You may want to do this as a Bible drill, having the person who found the verse first read it aloud.

3. When someone believes he or she knows what the game is about (feet and shoes), tell that person to keep it a secret until *all* the verses have been read. Then you might want to ask something

like this: **What did you find in all these verses? That's right—feet and shoes! Now, can you guess what game we're going to play? It's called the Shoe Game!**

4. Ask everyone to get three pairs of his or her own shoes.

5. Pile all the shoes in the middle of your family room floor and mix them up very well. Everyone should be barefooted or wearing socks.

6. Announce that we will be turning off the lights. When we do, that will be the signal for everyone to find *one matching pair of shoes* and put them on correctly. The winner is the first one to put a pair on correctly and yell "Shoes on!"

7. Have the children sit in a circle around the pile of shoes; then a parent should turn off the lights.

8. *Find those shoes!*

9. Repeat the game several times. It's fun!

SUGGESTIONS:

When Craig and I were in college, part of our initiation was a variation of this game, but then we had nearly *300* pairs of shoes in a pile—some pile! We did not have to find them in the dark, though, so we added *that* twist to make it more exciting.

What has been interesting is the way the game has changed over the years. When we first began doing this, the boys were both very small, and thus no one had a problem with mixing his or her shoes with someone else's. Later Robb's feet were near the same size as mine and we would constantly put on each other's shoes. (Dad and Jay could then easily win the game.)

Now, the game is indeed interesting, for Dad and Robb have about the same size shoes *and* Jay and I have the same size—so we all end up tugging and pulling on the same shoes. One of these days (in the not-too-far-distant future), *I* will have the smallest feet and I will once again be able to win!

Ten
HOLIDAYS AND SPECIAL EVENTS

NEW YEAR'S BLESSINGS

MATERIALS NEEDED:
- [ ] family candle and matches
- [ ] Bible
- [ ] a sheet of paper for each child in the family
- [ ] pen

TEXT: Genesis 48:8–49:28

PREPARATION:
- [ ] Read through Genesis 48:8–49:28 about the blessings that Jacob gave to his sons and Joseph's sons.
- [ ] You will be giving a blessing to each of your children, speaking of qualities that they possess and how God can use these qualities to glorify Him. Make sure that you do point out *qualities,* not abilities or talents. Craig decided to emphasize three qualities for each son, and then he wrote out (each on a separate piece of paper) these blessings:

To Robb,
  You are a person of responsibility and service. May God continue to give this to you and may He glorify Himself through it. May you be a great servant and leader for God. Remember, you will serve by leading and lead by being in submission to God and others. *May you have the strength and energy from God.*
  You are a person who loves life. May God give you the joy of

129

seeing the pleasure that God desires for us to enjoy in this life that He created for us. May the contentment that comes from knowing God fill your heart and soul. *May you have the joy of the Lord.*

You are your own person with God, not prone to follow the crowd, but to stand independently. May God continue to use this for His glory and may He always remind you that this is only possible by being the person God intends. *May you know God—then yourself.*

To Jay,

You are a creative person who sees things in new ways and in a new light. May God use this to help the church of God to be in fresh relationship with Him. May God grant you the privilege of using this freshness and creativity in your personal journey of faith with Him. *May you know God in new and deeper ways.*

You are a fun-loving person. May God grant you the joy of enjoying life as He created and intended. May you bring joy to others who need help in times of difficulty. May your fun-loving nature sustain you in times of challenge. *May you know the contentment of God.*

You are a sensitive, deeply feeling person. May God use this to make you very sensitive to His will and leading in your life. May He glorify Himself by using this to reveal Himself to others through your caring sensitivity. *May you be God's instrument to heal and comfort others.*

☐ Take time to prayerfully consider which qualities God would have you write about for your children, and then feel free to use these blessings as a pattern, if you wish.

FAMILY TIME:

1. Place your lighted family candle in the middle of your table.

2. Open with prayer by asking God to be with your family in a special way tonight.

3. Read Genesis 48:8–49:28 aloud.

4. Tell your children that just as Jacob pronounced a special blessing on his children, you would like to do so tonight. Explain

that the blessings will be about special qualities which God has granted each one and which you pray God will continue to use in the future.

5. Begin with your oldest child first and place your hand on his or her head as you read the blessing. Continue the same way for each child.

6. Close in prayer, thanking God for each special child (and that child's unique qualities) which He has given your family.

SUGGESTIONS:

We've often heard the adage that what you tell a child he or she will become will indeed come to pass. Therefore, if you tell a child that he will amount to nothing, the child will do just that. But if you emphasize qualities that God will use in the future, the child will work hard to make this come true. For this reason we constantly point out to our children those special qualities with which He has blessed them, and how He can use those unique qualities for His glory.

Please note again that we are *not* emphasizing beauty, intelligence, talents, and abilities. The world too often praises children for these—or shames them for their lack of beauty, brains, and talent. Instead, we want to focus on those inner qualities or gifts which make them unique and special people.

The boys' eyes took on a special glow in the candlelight when their dad read these blessings. It was a touching moment for all of us and one they have not quickly forgotten. These blessings are very important to them and I assume always will be. *This* type of inheritance has more worth than anything made of silver or gold. Lord, may it produce gold in our sons in the future.

VALENTINE HEARTS

MATERIALS NEEDED:

- [ ] Bible
- [ ] 3″ x 5″ file cards
- [ ] felt-tip pens (fine-tip)
- [ ] Scotch Tape
- [ ] red construction paper
- [ ] scissors
- [ ] pencils or pens
- [ ] a small cross (possibly one from a necklace)
- [ ] a small box, wrapping paper, and ribbon
- [ ] family candle and matches
- [ ] a candle for each member of the family

TEXT: 2 Corinthians 1:21-22

PREPARATION:

- [ ] Construct the table marker, writing out 2 Corinthians 1:21-22.
- [ ] Trace and cut out a heart from red construction paper for each member of the family.
- [ ] Think through qualities and talents that your children have; you may need to suggest these as "gifts" that they can give to God. For example, a child who plays an instrument can play it for God's glory. A ballplayer can be a leader who exemplifies Christ before his teammates.
- [ ] Wrap the cross in the box; make it as beautiful as possible.
- [ ] Place your family candle in the middle of the dining room table. Have the smaller candles (one for each person) ready and matches available. Hide the wrapped package within reach of the table.

FAMILY TIME:

1. Read 2 Corinthians 1:21-22 during dinner, and discuss the wonderful gift that God has given us (His Spirit in our hearts). Explain the analogy of the "deposit" by asking questions like:

- **What is a deposit? When do we put one down on something?** (when we see something we really desire)
- **Does that mean we are claiming the article as *ours?***
- **What is Christ claiming as His?** (Us!)
- **When will we be *fully* His?**

2. Later gather around the table and get out the wrapped package. Ask something like this: **In this package is the greatest gift that was *ever* given. Can anyone guess what it is?** Allow children to make guesses and then let them open the gift.

3. Explain that the cross represents Christ's very life as a sacrifice for our sins; later He would send His Spirit to fill our hearts as 2 Corinthians 1:21-22 says.

4. Announce that we have given a gift to Christ too—our hearts. But each day we need to continue committing our lives to Him, giving God our talents, abilities, and qualities to be used by Him.

5. Give everyone a candle, a red heart, and a pencil or pen.

6. Explain that each of us is to write on the red heart what ability, quality, or talent we intend to use to serve Him this year. (At this point you may need to give those suggestions to your children.) This is a *gift* we give to Christ. Be sure to have everyone write specifically *how* he or she will use this ability to serve.

7. Ask everyone to share his or her "gift" and light a candle while doing so.

8. Close in prayer by thanking God for His greatest gift to us—salvation.

SUGGESTIONS:

Even primary ages can understand using abilities and talents because "I love God and He gave me this ability." Therefore, this devotion can be adapted for younger children. Just be sure that you have several relatable examples (the abilities and specifically how they can be used to serve God) for them to choose from. They also will readily understand that the greatest gift ever given was Christ Himself.

A philosophy professor of ours drilled into us that we should do *everything* to the glory of God. Too often we separate "secular" from "spiritual" when God did not intend this. This devotion can teach children how *not* to draw "parentheses" around areas of their lives: they can seek to glorify God on the basketball court, at the piano, during Boy Scouts—any place and anytime.

Since God graciously gave us abilities and talents, we should use them whenever and wherever for His glory. If children can understand and apply this concept, they have the potential to become Christians who truly *live* their Christianity.

MOTHER'S DAY AND FATHER'S DAY

MATERIALS NEEDED:
- [ ] construction paper
- [ ] crepe paper streamers
- [ ] heavy cardboard
- [ ] gold wrapping paper
- [ ] felt-tip pens (fine-tip)
- [ ] crayons
- [ ] stapler and staples
- [ ] Scotch Tape
- [ ] masking tape
- [ ] scissors
- [ ] glue

PREPARATION:

[ ] Trace a crown (opened out) onto the cardboard; glue the gold wrapping paper onto the cardboard. Cut out the crown and staple and tape it closed.

[ ] With the construction paper and felt-tip pens, make a certificate for Father's Day which looks something like this:

WE DECLARE THAT DAD GETS
SUNDAY AFTERNOON OFF!

HAPPY FATHER'S DAY!   WE PROMISE!

_____

_____

_____
                                      signatures

WE LOVE YOU!

Or for Mother's Day:

WE DECLARE THAT MOM DOES NOT HAVE TO MAKE
SUPPER OR CLEAN HOUSE TODAY! DAD HAS TO MAKE
AND CLEAN UP SUPPER!! (WE KIDS WILL HELP TOO,
DAD.)

_____

_____

_____
                    signatures

☐ Allow your children to use their creativity to design and make their own unique certificate.

☐ Decorate Mom's or Dad's chair (depending on whether it's Mother's Day or Father's Day) at your table with the crepe paper streamers. Make it look as "royal" as possible.

☐ If your children desire, have them make cards from construction paper and felt-tip pens or crayons. From experience, I know that these are *much* more special than store-bought cards.

☐ You also may want to allow your children to make breakfast for Mom or Dad.

FAMILY TIME:
1. First thing in the morning—though not *too* early—children should greet the honored parent with "Happy Mother's/Father's Day! You are queen (or king) for a day!"
2. Take Mom or Dad to her or his "throne"—the decorated chair. Place the crown on his or her head and give out the certificates and cards. At this point you may want to serve the honored parent the breakfast meal too.
3. Enjoy fellowshipping together during breakfast, continuing preferential treatment of the parent. Make sure that the certificate signers honor their commitments.

SUGGESTIONS:

I judge that one of my responsibilities as a parent is to teach my sons how to treat their future wives. If I allow them to disrespect me or to take me for granted, then I'm certainly *not* helping their future spouses. Instead, I want them to open doors for me, answer my questions respectfully, and most importantly—treat me as someone special. Therefore I often demand this by insisting on an evening out on my birthday plus a birthday cake from a bakery(!). I also attempt to set an example by treating their dad as someone very special.

The boys have caught onto this idea so well; as a matter of fact, often now *they* are the ones who initiate the many surprises for the honored person. They loved decorating Dad's chair and have insisted on repeating this procedure. They even demanded that he wear a "Superdad" button to work! The certificates were their idea too. (Can you imagine how great that makes a parent feel at the end of a long week of parenting?)

I firmly believe that if we parents just take the initiative, guiding our children at first, they will respond with their *own* amazing creativity and initiative. Since each year gets better than the one before, I can hardly wait to see what our guys come up with this year.

RESURRECTION DAY THANK-YOU'S

MATERIALS NEEDED:
- [ ] Bible
- [ ] 3″ x 5″ file cards
- [ ] felt-tip pens (fine-tip)
- [ ] Scotch Tape
- [ ] several sheets of notebook paper (If your children are older, you may want to use regular stationery.)
- [ ] pencils and pens
- [ ] construction paper
- [ ] stapler and staples
- [ ] family candle and matches

TEXTS: Matthew 27:1–28:10; Mark 16; Luke 24:1-12; John 20:1-18 (You will need to read through these and select the combination of verses that is best for your family. You may need to consult additional resources to understand the time framework of the Resurrection events; remember the list of helps available at the end of this book.)

PREPARATION:

[ ] Construct the table marker, writing out Mark 16:1-7 or any other combination of verses that you desire.

[ ] Study the Scripture passages on Christ's death and resurrection; choose and mark the verses you will read to your family later. Keep in mind attention span and what might be of special interest to your children.

[ ] You may also want to do some research on burial procedures, embalming, and the tombs of biblical times. Again, consult helps at the end of this book.

[ ] Make a large envelope out of a sheet of construction paper by folding it over, allowing enough to overlap for a flap to seal. Staple the edges. Write on the envelope: "Thank-you's to Jesus, (print the date)."

[ ] Place the family candle in the center of your dining room table. Have matches, the stapler, notebook paper, pens, and pencils ready for later.

FAMILY TIME:

1. During dinner have your children take turns reading the Scripture verses. You may want to discuss what a tomb was like, burial procedures, and embalming in biblical times. Since much of this is so foreign for today, this can be of great help to your children's understanding of the empty tomb and burial cloths.

2. Later gather around the table and light your family candle.

3. Open with prayer.

4. Read the Scripture passages which you have chosen, or you may choose to have your whole family take turns reading so that you may cover a larger section of Scripture.

5. Take time to discuss these beautiful passages. You may want to ask questions like:

- **How do you think Mary felt when she looked in the tomb? How did Peter feel?**
- **Notice that the angel tells them not to be frightened. Why do you suppose they were afraid?**
- **What did the angel then tell them to do?** (go and tell)
- **What should we do today?** (go and tell)

6. Announce that because of Jesus' great sacrifice of His life for us, you want to take time to write a very special thank-you to Him. You may want to preface this activity by asking this question: **Since we write thank-you's for presents from relatives and friends, shouldn't we also write a thank-you for the greatest gift we have ever received?**

7. Hand out notebook paper and pens or pencils to everyone. Explain that family members will be writing a thank-you letter to Jesus, thanking Him for dying on the cross for their sins. Encourage family members to make the letter personal by saying exactly why they are thankful this year, explaining what His death and resurrection means to them. Ask them to address it "Dear Jesus" and sign the letter with a signature and date. Have everyone fold his or her letter when finished.

8. Collect the letters without reading them, and put them in the envelope that you made earlier. Staple it closed and announce that you will put this away for next year. At that time next year you will open the envelope, read these thank-you's aloud, and then write new ones for the *coming year.* This way you have something very

special to look forward to on Resurrection Day next year.

9. Close in prayer, thanking God for His Son's loving and sacrificial death and resurrection.

SUGGESTIONS:

When we celebrate Resurrection Day this year, it will be our third year to write these thank-you's to Jesus. The first time we wrote them was fun, but opening the ones composed one long year ago was even more enjoyable! Somehow, waiting that year added to the suspense—and besides, we had forgotten what we had written, so they were nearly a complete surprise. I tell you this to encourage you *not* to yield to the temptation to read those letters right away.

Hopefully, these letters will also become treasured memories and a type of journal recording our sons' spiritual maturity. As the years go by, I pray the thank-you's evidence the growth we so desire for them. And if we as parents enjoy seeing the spiritual journey occur, imagine what these letters will mean to the children themselves over the years to adulthood.

Every year we plan to read each set of thank-you's. As the stack grows, we'll be piling up memories upon memories, building another bonding family tradition. But most of all we pray that our Lord truly will be worshiped and adored by our family through this simple and yet sincere offering to Him.

CHILDREN'S DAY

MATERIALS NEEDED:
- [ ] Bible
- [ ] 3″ x 5″ file cards
- [ ] felt-tip pens (fine-tip)
- [ ] Scotch Tape
- [ ] construction paper
- [ ] small surprises as gifts for your children
- [ ] wrapping paper and ribbon
- [ ] a free day so you can take your children to a zoo, museum, park, or somewhere else which interests them

TEXT: Psalm 127:3-5

PREPARATION:
- [ ] Construct the table marker, writing out Psalm 127:3-5.
- [ ] Buy and wrap small gifts that your children will enjoy.
- [ ] Plan a day of fun for your children (preferably the closest day to their last day of school for the year) at a zoo, park, or museum. Take a picnic lunch if possible, complete with favorite treats!
- [ ] Make a card for each child that says "Happy Children's Day!" Fold construction paper in half and decorate the cards as you desire. Inside you may want to put sentiments that say something like this:

> We know you've worked
> Really hard this year,
> And you deserve a rest.
> So we declare this
> "Children's Day"
> With *fun* the only test!

Or:

> Since today is your last day
> For trudging off to school,

We've declared this "Children's Day"
And *fun's* our only rule!

Sometimes parents may want to write a more serious sentiment, listing accomplishments each child has made in school that year and describing the parents' pride in each child's hard work, determination, and responsibility. Be careful, though, that what you express is indeed true. You may want to keep the sentiment light if one of your children has had a rough year. Remember that you need to compliment the qualities *behind* the grades—determination, hard work, responsibility, not giving up. Grades should be pointed out as a less important representation of these more significant inner motivations.

☐ You may also want to make cupcakes or a cake decorated with "Happy Children's Day," or other treats that your children especially like. Prepare a picnic if possible.

FAMILY TIME:

1. Greet your children first thing in the morning with a cheerful "Happy Children's Day!" You might want to answer their "What's *that?*" with the explanation that since we have a Mother's and Father's Day, we decided that we needed a Children's Day too.

2. Give them their cards and presents—plus a big hug and kiss, of course.

3. Point out the table marker, reading the verses to your children. Tell them that God says that children are a *blessing* to a family and that you are especially blessed to have them!

4. Announce to them that this day will be dedicated to them and fun activities for the entire family. Tell them where you'll be going and pack the picnic lunch and family into the car.

5. Enjoy this very special day!

SUGGESTIONS:

The first year that we invented "Children's Day," a special light came into our kids' eyes—that sparkle that says, "You think I'm special and that makes me feel wonderful!" (I do enjoy seeing that twinkle!) I believe that instituting this day said to them that they were just as important to this family as a mother and father; we need and love them and in this way we can say thankyou—just as we do on Mother's and Father's Days.

They were thrilled with the cards and presents, but they most appreciated the gift of *ourselves* and our *time*. We reserved an entire day to celebrate *them*. Can you imagine what that does for a child's feelings of worth?

Our Children's Day memories include delicious picnic lunches and visiting several different types of interesting museums. And honestly, Craig and I have enjoyed those days as much or more than our sons. I'll let you in on one secret we've kept, though: since we're celebrating getting *out* of school, we dare not tell them that going to a museum is educational!

PREPARING FOR VACATION—BURYING THE GROUCH!

MATERIALS NEEDED:
- [ ] an old, dirty sock (the yuckier, the better!)
- [ ] a spade for digging
- [ ] cardboard
- [ ] construction paper
- [ ] felt-tip pens (broad- and fine-tip) or crayons
- [ ] 3″ x 5″ file cards
- [ ] Scotch Tape
- [ ] scissors

PREPARATION:

- [ ] Construct the table marker, if desired. You may want to write out something fun like, "Vacation time!" or, "Here we come, _____(destination)_____ !" Or you could drop a hint about the dirty sock by writing, "What does a *dirty sock* have to do with our *vacation?*"

- [ ] Make a "tombstone" by cutting the cardboard into the correct shape. Cover it with construction paper.

- [ ] Have felt-tip pens (or crayons) ready for decorating the tombstone later. Set aside the dirty sock and spade.

FAMILY TIME:

1. During dinner, build curiosity by discussing your vacation, or if you have written "What does a *dirty sock* have to do with our *vacation?*" on the table marker, ask them to attempt to figure out the riddle. (It will be quite interesting to hear what answers they come up with!)

2. Later announce solemnly that you will be having a funeral and burial for "the Grouch." Explain that the Grouch is an old, dirty sock and it represents all of the grumping that family members might be tempted to do on your vacation. And once you have buried that sock, the Grouch will be *dead.*

3. Get out the cardboard tombstone and felt-tip pens or crayons. Allow everyone to write sayings or color the tombstone as he or she wishes. You may want to put a poem like this on your tombstone:

Here lies our old, dirty sock;
Never again will it walk.
We named it the Grouch
And for this we vouch—
Our speech will be kind when we talk!

4. Take the tombstone, sock, and spade to your backyard. Dig a small hole and, with much ceremonial aplomb, deposit the Grouch into the hole and cover it with dirt.

5. Place the tombstone at the top of the hole. Remind everyone again that *the Grouch has been buried* and therefore there will be no need for grumping during our vacation.

6. As an added incentive, announce that *whoever does grouch the most during the trip will receive the dug-up sock as a special gift from the family.* (Remind them too how clean and sweet-smelling it will be by then!)

7. Enjoy your family vacation, slipping in constant reminders by saying things like: "Was that a grumpy response? Sounds like he wants the Grouch when we get home!"

SUGGESTIONS:

Craig used this ceremony when he was a youth pastor and the Senior High youth group went on a long trip. The results were amazing; attitudes adjusted immediately when the kids thought about that disgusting sock. (Craig *did* present it as a necklace to the honored recipient at the Sunday evening service.)

When our kids got older and we were contemplating a long road trip and the endless arguments coming from the backseat, we pulled out the Grouch idea to be used for our family. Again it worked marvelously well. All we had to do was *hint* about that sock—a particularly gross specimen—and *everyone* (including Mom and Dad) shaped up quickly. In fact, the subject of grumping became a fun one as we teased endlessly about Dad's stinky sock!

Though we never intended to actually dig up that old sock, which was definitely better left buried, we found that we wouldn't have needed to anyway. The mere threat of being awarded the Grouch was enough to keep each one of us at least *reasonably* pleasant for the entire vacation.

BACK TO SCHOOL

MATERIALS NEEDED:

☐ Bibles for each family member
☐ 3″ x 5″ file cards
☐ felt-tip pens (fine-tip)
☐ Scotch Tape
☐ back-to-school gifts for your children—possibly a new backpack, crayons, hat and mittens, etc.
☐ scissors
☐ wrapping paper and ribbon

TEXT: 2 Corinthians 4:8-10, 15-16.

PREPARATION:

☐ Study 2 Corinthians 4:8-16 and the background of this passage. Consult the list of helps at the back of this book. Note that the thrust of this chapter is that we should not lose heart; we should never get so discouraged that we quit.

☐ You may want to teach your children the meaning of these words also:

1. *hard-pressed*—afflicted, pressured
2. *perplexed*—without a way, confused, at a loss
3. *persecuted*—to be pursued or attacked
4. *struck-down*—thrown down, shoved aside, cast off

☐ Wrap the back-to-school presents for your children, and hide them wherever the end of their "Clue Hunt" will be.

☐ Plan your Clue Hunt. I used verses which gave clues for the *next* place to search for a clue. I wrote just the references on the cards so that they had to look up the verses and read them aloud. These were the references on each card:

1. Psalm 19:6 (This clue was for the *furnace.*)
2. Matthew 9:6 (the welcome mat)
3. Psalm 6:6 (our bed)
4. 1 Peter 2:21 (the steps)
5. Leviticus 15:5 (the clothes washer)
6. Matthew 6:6 (the boys' room door)
7. Isaiah 21:5 (kitchen table)

8. Ecclesiastes 9:4 (our dog's bed)

9. Matthew 10:42 (the refrigerator, where we hid the boys' presents!)

Caution: Make sure that you save the first clue to give to your children; hide the remaining ones in order so that Matthew 9:6 is *on the furnace,* Psalm 6:6 is *under the welcome mat,* etc. Tape the clues down carefully so that they do not get misplaced.

FAMILY TIME:

1. During dinner, take turns reading the verses on the table marker. At this time you may want to discuss the hardships that going back to school will inevitably bring. Emphasize that the thrust of this passage is that we should not lose heart and give up. Also discuss the fun and exciting events of attending school. Be sure to end your discussion on an "up" note.

2. Later open your family time with prayer.

3. Read 2 Corinthians 4:8-10 and 15-16 again and explain to your children the meaning of the words *hard-pressed, perplexed, persecuted,* and *struck-down.* Use this discussion as a time to reinforce the positive side—that we are not crushed, not in despair, not abandoned, and not destroyed for *He is with us!* And we never lose heart or quit, for "inwardly we are being renewed day by day" (v. 16b).

[handwritten margin note: exam. of Rusty in Back Home]

4. Point out also that verse 15 gives such promise and hope. Here we're told the maturing process is "for our benefit" and that the result is thanksgiving overflowing "to the glory of God."

5. For application, you may want to ask questions like:

- **When are some of the specific times you may feel hard-pressed, perplexed, persecuted, or struck-down?** (during homework or tests, when another student makes fun of me, when I'm extremely tired)
- **What should your response be?** (to not lose heart)
- **What are some things we might be thankful for in the midst of these troubles?** (that *God* is in control, that I can be a testimony to Him by not seeking revenge, by *not giving up!*)

6. To liven things up a bit, announce that now you'll have a Clue Hunt with very special surprises at the end of the trail. Ask your

children to first get their Bibles. Then explain the procedure: you will give them the first clue; they must look up the verse, read it aloud, and figure out what clue it gives to find the *next* clue's hiding place. At the end of their hunt, they'll find special back-to-school gifts.

7. When your children have found their presents, close in prayer, asking God to continue encouraging them so that they will not lose heart.

SUGGESTIONS:

Each year we attempt to send our children back to school with our encouragement, blessing, and a reminder that we will *always* be supporting them in prayer. For some reason I always feel a need to give them a special boost—a type of spiritual renewing for the long year ahead. Yes, the year will have times of fun, but it will also have its times of discouragement. It's *these* times that we need to prepare for.

Since we do need to buy those endless school supplies anyway, why not make this special and more fun by adding the excitement of a Clue Hunt? Our boys always love this, no matter what is at the end of the hunt. I wonder what they would do if I put *spinach* at the end?

HALLOWEEN PARTY

MATERIALS NEEDED:

- ☐ old articles of clothing: two large pairs of men's pants, two shirts, two ties (as wild as possible), two pairs of large-sized boots, two hats, and two sport coats, if possible
- ☐ apples and a large pan of water
- ☐ caramels, sticks, and apples to make caramel apples
- ☐ soda crackers
- ☐ bubble gum
- ☐ pumpkins, pencil, and a knife for carving

PREPARATION:

☐ Assemble the clothing for a relay race. Put one pair of pants, boots, a shirt, tie, sport coat, and hat in a large sack for the Orange Team; put the other set of clothing in a sack for the Black Team. Label the sacks "Orange Team" and "Black Team." First, though, make sure that the biggest person in the family *will* be able to put on each article of clothing!

☐ Prepare to bob for apples by washing the apples and putting them in a large pan of water.

☐ Get soda crackers and bubble gum ready for a "bubble gum relay."

☐ Buy your pumpkins for carving. We always make a special outing to pick out our pumpkins. Every year each of us has very different tastes for what constitutes the *perfect* pumpkin.

☐ Set aside an apple for each member of the family, plus caramels and Popsicle sticks to make caramel apples.

FAMILY TIME:

1. After supper gather your family for a family game night. Divide into two teams and assign names—Orange and Black if you desire, or allow teams to make up their own creative names. If you don't have enough family members to make two teams, you can adapt and enjoy the games anyway.

2. While parents still have stamina and plenty of energy, do the "Hobo Relay." Put the sacks of clothes several yards away from the

starting line. Have team members line up behind the starting line. At the "Ready, set, . . . go!" signal, the first team member should race to the sack and bring it back to his or her team. He or she should then put on the entire set of clothes, run back to where the sack was, and back again to the team to remove the clothes. Then the next team member in line should repeat the process. (NOTE: Other team members can help dress and undress their teammates.)

3. The winning team is the first one to complete the relay (for each team member) and return the clothes to the sack. You may want to declare them "Honorary Hobos!"

4. Allow everyone to bob for an apple. (You may want to use your apple to make the caramel apple later.)

5. Hand out soda crackers and bubble gum to everyone. Announce that all team members must eat a cracker and then blow a bubble. The first team to have each member blow a bubble wins!

6. Design faces on your pumpkins and then have *parents* carve them. You may want to put in candles and light them also.

7. Make caramel apples. Melt the caramels with a couple of teaspoons of water. Enjoy a gooey time of fellowship and fun together!

SUGGESTIONS:

Not too long ago, Halloween fell on a Wednesday night. We had always allowed the boys to dress up (though *not* in witches', ghosts', or any other satanic characters' costumes) and visit friends' houses. But this particular year presented a problem. We wanted the boys to learn that commitments to church activities were more important than Halloween fun, but we also did not want them to resent attending church. Therefore, we came up with what turned out to be a very fun compromise.

On the night before Halloween, we told the boys that we would have a party as a family that would be just as much fun—or more so—than trick-or-treating would be. We planned as many fun games as we could think of, plus plenty of delicious treats, and we had a ball together. They didn't miss the "normal" Halloween at all, and I expect they would choose to do this type of party every year if given the choice. And more importantly, they learned a valuable lesson about commitments and worshiping God—a lesson learned in the best way, for it was indeed fun.

THANKSGIVING COLLECTION

MATERIALS NEEDED:
- ☐ Bible
- ☐ 3″ x 5″ file cards
- ☐ felt-tip pens (fine-tip)
- ☐ Scotch Tape
- ☐ a small paper bag for each member of the family

TEXT: Psalm 100

PREPARATION:
- ☐ Construct the table marker, writing out Psalm 100.
- ☐ Prepare the paper bags by writing each family member's name (in felt-tip pen) on a bag.

FAMILY TIME:

1. During dinner have your children take turns reading Psalm 100.

2. Discuss the psalm by asking questions like:

- ⦿ **What are the main themes of this psalm?** (praise of thankfulness to God; worship with joy; He has made us and therefore we are His; He is a God of goodness, love, and faithfulness—all reasons to praise Him!)

- ⦿ **How does this psalm make you feel?** (thankful, joyful, happy)

- ⦿ **Can you see why this is a perfect psalm for Thanksgiving?** (That is exactly the response the psalmist intended from his listeners.)

3. Begin your family time with prayer by asking God to give you all thankful hearts and a good time of fellowship together. (You probably will want to meet around your dining table.)

4. Reread Psalm 100 and then give a bag to each member of the family.

5. Explain that these bags will be used by each one to gather a "Thanksgiving Collection." Everyone is to collect representations of things for which he or she is thankful. You may need to give some examples to help your children get started. Some suggestions are: a

candle from earlier devotions to represent the family, a vitamin to stand for good health, or a key to the house to represent your home.

6. Ask everyone to collect as many things as he or she wishes to put into the bag. Tell them they have about ten minutes and then family members will meet around the table again to share their collections with each other.

7. After ten minutes (or whenever everyone is ready), gather around the table. You may want to allow the youngest member of the family to go first and then proceed by ages. Be sure to express excitement and support for each child as he or she shares a collection; this will help the child to be open and enthusiastic concerning his or her items.

8. When everyone has shown his or her collection, you may want to reread Psalm 100 once more and then close with sentence prayers. (See the devotional entitled *Sentence Prayers* for instructions.) In this way everyone can then thank God for the blessings He has abundantly provided.

make beeswax candles for gifts

SUGGESTIONS:

Though younger children may need some help to find representations of things for which they are thankful, they can fully participate in this family time. They probably have covered the topic of thankfulness several times at church, and thus they should be excited about collecting their ideas.

Parents, remember that their conceptualizing of *what* they are thankful for will be quite different from yours. Children probably will think about family, but don't be surprised if the dog (or cat, hamster, goldfish) is next on the list! Realize that this is quite appropriate for their age abilities, and *do not* scold them if they should not remember certain things, such as the Bible.

Our family enjoyed collecting these representations of treasures and then sharing the items afterward. Again, our sons did a wonderful job and even remembered to be thankful for things that *I* had not thought about.

Now, my special thanks go to Grammy (my special mom!), who gave me this idea for a family time that was fun and a helpful reminder of our many blessings too.

CHRISTMAS CELEBRATION

MATERIALS NEEDED:

- ☐ Bible
- ☐ 3″ x 5″ file cards
- ☐ felt-tip pen (fine-tip)
- ☐ Scotch Tape
- ☐ musical instruments, if any members of your family play
- ☐ Christmas music, if possible
- ☐ the family candle plus any other Christmas candles you may have
- ☐ a small candle (to be held) for each member of the family
- ☐ matches

TEXTS: Matthew 1:18–2:12; Luke 2:1-10

PREPARATION:

☐ Construct the table marker, writing out the angel's message found in Luke 2:10-14: "But the angel said to them, 'Do not be afraid. I bring you good news of great joy'" and so forth.

☐ Ask your children to be in charge of the music for the evening. They will need to choose which carols they wish to sing (from a hymnal, if you have one) and practice any songs that they want to sing or play on an instrument. For example, if one of your children plays an instrument, whether it be a piano, violin, or flute, you may want to suggest that he or she play a carol while the other brothers and sisters sing along. Or you may have two children who play who could perform a duet. Allow them to be creative in whatever they decide to do. Ask them to write down the order of the music, so they won't leave anyone or anything out!

☐ Decide on a sharing question that has a Christmas theme. Some of the questions that we have used are:

- **Why is this particular Christmas special to me?**
- **Why do I especially appreciate Christ's coming to earth this year?**
- **What have I learned about Christ during this holiday season?**
- **Why am I thankful for Christmas this year?**

- **How have I changed since last Christmas? What does this say about my walk with God?**

  ☐ Place the Christmas candles around your living room. Have the other candles (that you will be holding) and matches ready. You may wish to put the family candle in the most conspicuous spot—at the center of the fireplace mantel, for example.

  ☐ Practice reading the Christmas story so that you can read it with excitement and inflection—and by candlelight too!

FAMILY TIME:

1. During dinner you may want to discuss topics like: **What was your favorite gift that you received for Christmas? What was the best gift that you have ever *given* for Christmas? What is your favorite Christmas memory? What do you remember as being the best memory of last Christmas?**

2. Later, when it's dark and the candlelight is most effective, light all of the candles, except the individual candles. Turn out all electric lights, if possible.

3. Begin with prayer by thanking God for this beautiful season of the year. You may want to mention also that your desire is to concentrate on the *true* meaning of Christmas—Jesus Christ.

4. A parent should then read the Christmas story from the Gospels of Matthew and Luke.

5. Ask your children to lead you in worshiping Jesus through music. If they do not include many Christmas carols, add some of the well-known ones such as "Silent Night," "O Little Town of Bethlehem," "Joy to the World," "Away in a Manger," and "The First Noel."

6. Give every member of the family a candle.

7. Announce that you will now have a time of sharing and that as each one shares, that person should light his or her candle from the family candle. (Little ones will of course need help with this.)

8. Give the sharing questions. You may want to ask two or three questions and allow everyone to answer one or more of his or her choosing.

9. Sing one or two of your family's favorite carols.

10. Close with prayer, thanking God for the gift of your family and most importantly, His Son.

SUGGESTIONS:

When our children were still very young, Craig and I decided that we wanted to begin several special Christmas traditions. Some are just fun, like the yearly friendly Mom and Dad hassle over the *perfect* Christmas tree. (You know how it goes—I find the best tree after *much* looking, and *he* thinks it's too big!) But other traditions are meant to do one thing only: keep us concentrating on the real meaning of Christmas—worshiping Jesus Christ.

To teach our children *how* to worship and to not get totally caught up in all the excitement of gifts has always been a challenge. We knew our focus for Christmas Eve then would have to be a worship time that would pull us all emotionally and thoughtfully toward Him. Therefore we added the candles, which add tremendously to a worshipful atmosphere, and a question for sharing that encourages all of us to think about Christ and what He has done for us.

This format *has* been successful for us, and I believe each of us now considers this one of our favorite family traditions. I know that watching the candles being reflected in my family's eyes always brings a stirring response from me of appreciation and love for my Lord. If our sons experience just a fraction of what I feel during this family time, then I know that we have kept our eyes on what should be the *focus* of this season—Jesus Christ.

SPIRITUAL BIRTHDAYS

MATERIALS NEEDED:
- ☐ Bible
- ☐ 3″ x 5″ file cards
- ☐ felt-tip pens (fine-tip)
- ☐ Scotch Tape
- ☐ gifts for the birthday child (You may want to get one for fun and one especially for a *spiritual* birthday, such as a devotional book or novel from a Christian book publisher, a Christian musical tape, a poster with Scripture on it, etc.)
- ☐ wrapping paper and ribbon
- ☐ birthday cake, candles, and matches
- ☐ a cross-stitch, calligraphy, or printed Scripture verse chosen especially for the child, if possible (You will also need a frame.)

TEXT: Choose a verse or verses for your child. We chose verses which spoke to our children's strengths and/or weaknesses. If your child has already spoken of a favorite verse, you may wish to use this. Spend some time in prayer before deciding.

PREPARATION:
- ☐ Construct the table marker, writing out "Happy Spiritual Birthday, _____*(name)*_____!" or "This Is _____*(name)*_____'s Special Day!"
- ☐ Make a cake, complete with "Happy Spiritual Birthday, _____*(name)*_____!" and candles.
- ☐ Choose a verse that might comfort your child or point out one of his or her strengths or help with a weakness, or just one that you think "fits" that special child. We chose Joshua 1:9 for our elder son because of the strength of the command and because of the comfort found there ("for the Lord your God will be with you wherever you go"). For our younger son we chose 1 Peter 5:6-7, which includes commands as well as comfort. (I especially like the alternate translation that says, "for you are His personal concern.") Consult your concordance or resources for help. Be sure to spend

time in prayer before making this important decision.

☐ After choosing the verse for your child, you may want to use cross-stitch, calligraphy, or printing to frame the Scripture passage. (This makes a very special present that you will want to wrap, also.)

☐ Wrap the birthday presents.

FAMILY TIME:

1. During supper encourage the child to give his or her testimony. You may not want to use the phrase "give a testimony" as this could be threatening. Instead, simply ask the child to tell what happened on the day that he or she was saved. You might want to ask questions like: **Exactly what did you do and say? How did you feel *before* you were saved? How did you feel afterward? Can you tell us how you've changed since that important day?** Allow your child to be the center of attention as this important story is retold!

2. After supper serve the cake with lighted candles. And don't forget to sing "Happy Birthday to You!"

3. Bring out the presents, saving the framed Scripture verse for last.

4. When your child opens the framed verse, you may want to say something like: **This is our special gift to you—a verse that we want you to memorize and keep in your heart forever. We picked it especially for you because we believe it will help you to serve God better. Always remember how much we love you! We are so very happy that you have Jesus in your heart and that we can celebrate the anniversary of that most important day. May this Scripture verse always be special to you and a remembrance of this spiritual birthday.**

5. Close with a special prayer of dedication for the birthday child. Be sure to thank God that this child is His and ask for continued spiritual growth over the next year.

SUGGESTIONS:

To do this devotional you obviously must first have a child who has been saved, and secondly, you need to know the date on which he or she became a Christian. If you do not know the exact day, try to figure out the *nearest* date and assign this as your child's spiritual birth date.

This celebration has so many good things to offer for not only the birthday child, but also for the entire family. When someone retells his or her testimony, the person is built up by the reminder of the work which God has accomplished. Others are edified by the testimony of salvation and growth since that time. And this should be such a joyous celebration, one of worship and praise to our God for what He has done.

Also, giving a child a life's verse can make a tremendous impact. Our sons memorized theirs quickly, and we have quoted them to each other during frightening, hurtful, and happy times. Remember too that a child will attempt to fulfill what the parents have predicted; by pointing out leadership and caring principles in their verses, we pray that our sons will indeed *become* these future spiritual leaders.

ANNIVERSARY QUIZ

MATERIALS NEEDED:
- [ ] Bible
- [ ] 3″ x 5″ file cards
- [ ] felt-tip pens (fine-tip)
- [ ] Scotch Tape
- [ ] several sheets of notebook paper
- [ ] pencils or pens
- [ ] the family candle (preferably your wedding candle) and matches
- [ ] pictures of you (Mom and Dad) during dating and engagement

TEXT: Ephesians 5:22-25, 28

PREPARATION:

- [ ] Construct the table marker, writing out Ephesians 5:22-25, 28.

- [ ] Study this passage by consulting Bible study notes and commentaries. (See the list at the end of this book.) Be prepared to explain to your children what "be subject to" and "head of the wife" mean and also more about the analogy of the husband loving the wife as Christ loves the church. Also be prepared to give specific examples of how you both demonstrate love toward each other.

- [ ] Collect an assortment of pictures from your dating and engagement years that you would like to show your children.

- [ ] Make up an anniversary quiz concerning your dating and engagement. Use this to teach your children about your commitment to your relationship, as a time for your children to get to know you better (as *people* instead of just parents), and as a way to show them God's ideas for love and marriage in action. Be sure to add a touch of humor too! Our quiz went like this:

1. On our first date we went:
   a. to a movie
   b. for a walk
   c. to a basketball game
   d. to a freshman class function

2. On our second date we went:
   a. to a movie
   b. for a walk
   c. to a basketball game
   d. to a freshman class function
3. What words best describe our first kiss?
   a. quickie
   b. long and romantic
   c. unusual
   d. not memorable!
4. We played an unusual game with a:
   a. kite
   b. nut
   c. pen and paper
   d. stuffed bear
5. Every Wednesday we ate for supper:
   a. steak and potatoes
   b. bologna sandwiches and taco chips
   c. hamburgers
   d. tuna noodle casserole
6. Daddy asked me to marry him how long after we began dating?
   a. three months
   b. six months
   c. nine months
   d. twelve months
7. In what location did he ask me?
   a. by a creek
   b. outside the dorm
   c. while walking
   d. in the car
8. What position was he in?
   a. on his knees
   b. standing
   c. sitting
   d. crawling
9. What position was *I* in?
   a. running away!

      b. walking

      c. standing still, in his arms

      d. sitting, in his arms

10. What exactly did he say?

      a. Will you marry me?

      b. Will you be my wife?

      c. Will you marry me in three years?

      d. Will you do me the honor of marrying me?

11. What did *I* say?

      a. Yes, sir!

      b. No way!

      c. Maybe

      d. Yes!

12. What month was this?

      a. January

      b. February

      c. March

      d. April

13. What month did I receive a diamond?

      a. June

      b. July

      c. August

      d. September

14. How long will I love Daddy (and Daddy love me)?

      a. forever

      b. to eternity

      c. always

      d. all of the above!

☐ Use this pattern to create a personalized and unique quiz about *your* romantic past (*and* present)!

FAMILY TIME:

1. During dinner have your children read the verses from Ephesians. Then share with them what you have learned from commentaries. Allow them to ask questions. Some you may anticipate are:

- **Does that mean Dad can boss Mom around all the time?**
- *How* **can Dad love Mom like Christ loved the church?**
- *How* **can Dad love Mom as his own body?**

Lastly, ask your children *how* Mom demonstrates subjection and how Dad demonstrates his love. (Give your examples too.)

2. Later announce that you will be giving a quiz to everyone (the other parent too) about your dating and engagement. Assure them that no grades will be given; this is just for fun!

3. Hand out paper and pencils to record answers. Give the quiz and enjoy their laughter and puzzlement. When you are finished, go back and give the correct answers, supplying more information about yourselves as you proceed. Share the pictures from dating and engagement years.

4. Close in prayer by thanking God for the institution of marriage and in particular for *your* marriage and family.

SUGGESTIONS:

If you have not noticed this already, children are generally fascinated with the stories concerning their parents' dates, engagement, and wedding. Our sons thoroughly enjoy hearing our humorous stories and especially the gooey, *romantic* ones! That may sound strange, but I think it's directly related to their need for security in Mom and Dad's love for each other—past and present. The more we reassure them that our love began with commitment (and is *not* based merely on feelings) and continues to grow stronger every year, the more secure our children will be. They desperately need to know that Mom and Dad love each other.

When I announced that I would be giving a quiz, both boys complained loudly that it wasn't fair for they wouldn't know all the answers and *Dad would.* I reassured them not to worry for it was just for fun. "And besides," I said, with a teasing glare at Craig, "I *expect* you two to miss some. If Dad misses *any,* he's in deep trouble!"

Completing this book on family devotions has been challenging, an enormous amount of work, distracting (here I am writing on the family and I keep getting aggravated at my family for interrupting me), and tremendously rewarding. We have so many wonderful memories tucked away; it is with joy that I recall those fun, warm, worshipful, sometimes frustrating, and loving times spent as a family. And that was a constant motivation, for I want you to store up these same types of memories!

Often when I present this material I hear the same response: "Well, we can't do this because. . . . " Parents seem to concentrate on the negative side—how these will be difficult to use—rather than the positive response of, "It will be hard, but we're willing to give it a try!" Yes, finding time and energy to have family times together *is* difficult but not impossible. Yes, you may have children of varying ages, but you can adapt, and children can be extremely flexible. Yes, it is hard to begin an entirely new format, but your children may be incredibly interested in something this unique. You will never know whether or not family devotions will work for you *unless you give it a chance.*

My family has prayed for this book from the initial idea through the last stage of production. Now we're praying for you and your loved ones. We're asking that you'll grow closer to God and each other, finding true joy in Him and your family. Now you've got plenty of devotional ideas and the prayers of Craig, Carolyn, Robb, and Jay behind you. Ready to begin?

Commentaries

The Bible Knowledge Commentary, New Testament. Walvoord, John F. and Roy B. Zuck, eds. Wheaton, Ill.: Victor Books, 1983.

The Bible Knowledge Commentary, Old Testament. Walvoord, John F. and Roy B. Zuck, eds. Wheaton, Ill.: Victor Books, 1985.

Tyndale New Testament Commentaries (multiple volumes). Morris, Leon, ed. Grand Rapids, Mich.: Eerdmans Publishing Co.

Tyndale Old Testament Commentaries (multiple volumes). Wiseman, D.J., ed. Downers Grove, Ill.: InterVarsity Press.

Introductions

A Popular Survey of the Old Testament. Geisler, Norman L. Grand Rapids, Mich.: Baker Book House, 1977.

A Survey of the New Testament, Revised Edition. Gundry, Robert H. Grand Rapids, Mich.: Zondervan Publishing House, 1981.

Concordances

The Contemporary Concordance of Bible Topics. Anderson, Ken. Wheaton, Ill.: Victor Books, 1988.

Nave's Topical Bible. Nave, Orville J. Chicago, Ill.: Moody Press, 1974.

Background Encyclopedias

The Illustrated Bible Dictionary (four volumes). Wheaton, Ill.: Tyndale House Publishers, 1980.

Manners and Customs of Bible Lands. Wright, Fred H. Chicago, Ill.: Moody Press, 1953.

The Victor Handbook of Bible Knowledge. Beers, Gilbert V. Wheaton, Ill.: Victor Books, 1981.

The Zondervan Pictorial Encyclopedia of the Bible (five volumes). Tenney, Merrill C., ed. Grand Rapids, Mich.: Zondervan Publishing House, 1975.

Bibles

The New International Version Study Bible. Barker, Kenneth, ed. Grand Rapids, Mich.: Zondervan Bible Publishers, 1985.

The New International Version Young Discoverer's Bible. Grand Rapids, Mich.: Zondervan Bible Publishers, 1985.

Recommended Reading

The Christmas Duck. Gire, Jr., Ken. Milford, Mich.: Mott Media, Inc., 1983.

The Lion, the Witch and the Wardrobe. Lewis, C.S. (This is *Book One in the Chronicles of Narnia;* there are seven in this series.) New York: Macmillan Pub. Co., 1950.

Love Comes Softly. Oke, Janette. (There are seven in this series.)

Minneapolis, Minn.: Bethany House Pub., 1979.

One-Eyed Cat. Fox, Paula. New York: Bradbury Press, 1984.

Tales of the Kingdom. Mains, David and Karen Mains. Elgin, Ill.: David C. Cook Pub. Co., 1983.

Tales of the Resistance. Mains, David and Karen Mains. Elgin, Ill.: David C. Cook Pub. Co., 1986.

When Calls the Heart. Oke, Janette. (There are four in this series.) Minneapolis, Minn.: Bethany House Pub., 1983.

A Wrinkle in Time. L'Engle, Madeleine. (This is followed by *A Wind in the Door* and *A Swiftly Tilting Planet.*) New York: Dell Pub. Co., Inc., 1976.

Subject	*Devotional Title*